KARL BARTH AND THE CHRISTIAN MESSAGE

KARL BARTH
AND THE CHRISTIAN MESSAGE

COLIN BROWN
Tutor, Tyndale Hall, Bristol

INTER-VARSITY PRESS
130 NORTH WELLS, CHICAGO, ILLINOIS 60606

© THE TYNDALE PRESS
First edition March 1967
Library of Congress Catalog Card Number 66–30696

Biblical quotations are from the Revised Standard Version. Copyright 1946 by the Division of Christian Education of the National Council of Churches of Christ in the USA.

COVER: The picture of Barth is based on a photograph by Maria Netter of Basle, as published by the Evangelischer Verlag A. G., Zollikon-Zürich, in the book *Antwort*, celebrating Barth's seventieth birthday in 1956.

Printed and Bound in Great Britain by
Bookprint Limited, London and Crawley

CONTENTS

ABBREVIATIONS

Antwort   *Antwort. Karl Barth zum siebzigsten Geburtstag am 10. Mai 1956* (Evangelischer Verlag,
Zollikon-Zürich, 1956).

Bettenson H. Bettenson (ed.), *Documents of the Christian
Church* (O.U.P., 1943, 1963²).

C.D.   Karl Barth, *Church Dogmatics* (T. & T. Clark,
1936–).

Denzinger H. Denzinger, *Enchiridion Symbolorum Defini-
tionum et Declarationum de Rebus Fidei et
Morum*, edited by C. Bannwart, J. B. Umberg
and K. Rahner (Herder, Freiburg, 1957³¹). (The
work is a collection of official pronouncements
of the Roman Catholic church. Numbers given
in reference refer to sections, not pages.)

Parrhesia *Parrhesia. Karl Barth zum achtzigsten Geburtstag am 10. Mai 1966* (Evangelischer Verlag,
Zürich, 1966).

R.R.   Karl Barth, *From Rousseau to Ritschl, being the
translation of eleven chapters of Die Protestantische Theologie im 19. Jahrhundert*, Eng. tr. by
B. Cozens, H. Hartwell and others (S.C.M. Press,
1959).

S.J.T.   *Scottish Journal of Theology.*

INTRODUCTION

Karl Barth is the great problem figure of contemporary theology. Conservatives mistrust him, suspecting that his neo-orthodoxy is somehow a cover for twisting truths that they hold vital and dear. Liberals raise their hats and look the other way. They either ignore, or, with Paul Tillich,[1] damn with faint praise, lauding his heroic defiance of the Nazis in the 1930s but dismissing his theology as irrelevant to the modern mind.

Yet there is probably no thinker today from whom more could be learnt, whether it be from his insights or from his mistakes. Barth has both on a grand scale. He is a theological Everest. He has not only written more than any other living theologian. His thought has a massive, lofty character which makes him tower high above the rank-and-file theological critic. Part of the reason for this is Barth's lifelong concern to grapple with the really big questions. He has never been one to be fobbed off with facile answers or to be carried away by the theological fashions of the hour. But the reason for Barth's eminence goes deeper. In part it may be accounted for by the way he enters into dialogue with the great thinkers of the past. To work one's way through Barth's major writings is to be brought into direct confrontation with the great exponents of Christianity like Luther and Calvin and also with its adversaries from the earliest heretics right down to present-day existentialist philosophers. Barth sees issues in breadth and depth. Above all, he brings to bear on them a profound and penetrating understanding of the Bible.

[1] *Ultimate Concern: Tillich in Dialogue*, edited by D. Mackenzie Brown (S.C.M. Press, 1965), pp. 63, 189f.

Even so, when all this has been said, it has to be admitted that great question-marks have been set against Barth's teaching. At certain points he seems to change the Christian message so as to make it mean almost the exact opposite of what it meant to its classical expositors of former centuries. At other points Barth is accused of purveying his own irrelevant brand of biblicism and irrationalism which, his accusers say, is useless to the honest inquirer today.

The aim of this study is neither to whitewash nor to condemn wholesale. Neither is it an attempt to map out Barth's teaching in all its ramifications. There are enough good books on the market which do this already.[2] Nor am I trying to contrast Barth's neo-orthodoxy with the older orthodoxy, so that at the end I can tell the reader which is the best buy. My aim is rather to try to get inside Barth's mind; to see the main issues as he sees them; to try to bring into critical focus Barth's approach to the Christian message. It is all too easy to get lost in Barth. His method of presentation, the complexity of his arguments and the sheer scale on which he operates often make it difficult to see the lie of the land. And yet there are certain basic themes which are easily overlooked but which give unity and dazzling simplicity to the whole. When these are grasped, the rest falls more easily into place. This study is concerned with the analysis and following out of these themes. It is by them that Barthianism as a theology stands or falls. It is by grappling with these key themes – whether or not we accept them in the way that Barth does – that we can learn most from Barth.

There are four main chapters in this study, plus a concluding summary. The first deals with what A. B. Come[3] and others have called Barth's 'Theological Pilgrimage'. It is an attempt to trace the course of Barth's life, to give some idea of his main writings, and to see how and why Barth has come to believe what he believes and think in the way that he does. Chapters 2, 3 and 4 examine three key areas of Barth's thought.

Chapter 2 on 'The Word of God and the Knowledge of

[2] See below, pp. 154–159.
[3] *An Introduction to Barth's Dogmatics for Preachers* (S.C.M. Press, 1963), pp. 23–67.

God' looks at Barth's answer to the central question of contemporary theology: How do we know God? We shall examine first Barth's reply – that we know God only through
God's revelation of Himself in His Word as witnessed to by
the Scriptures. Then we shall turn to some of the burning
questions raised by this reply: What is revelation? What is
the place of the Bible? What is the connection between personal encounter with God's Word in Christ and the words
of Scripture? How is it that events of the past can matter for
us today? Finally, we shall see how Barth's understanding of
revelation leads directly to the doctrine of the Trinity. For
revelation is none other than the work of God Himself,
Father, Son and Holy Spirit.

Chapter 3 is entitled 'The Bankruptcy of Natural Theology'. Put in their simplest terms, the questions here are:
Do we know God only through Christ and the gospel? Or
is there some alternative route to God via reason, nature or
general experience? Barth says Yes to the first question and
No to the second. Clearly he is swimming against the stream
of much modern Christian and non-Christian thought. It is
fashionable today to shrink from making exclusive claims on
behalf of the gospel. In this chapter we shall try to probe
the reasons why Barth and his opponents have reached these
opposite conclusions.

Chapter 4 looks at 'Barth's Christ-centred Approach to
God, Creation and Reconciliation'. Here we turn to some of
the questions which have occupied Barth's mind for the past
thirty or so years. Barth sees Jesus Christ as the key to the
whole of reality. He is not only the mediator and revealer.
Barth insists that we must understand every Christian doctrine in the light of Jesus Christ. The purpose of this chapter is to appreciate and assess three central doctrines in the
light of his understanding of Christ: the doctrines of God,
creation and reconciliation.

Taken together, these three main topics of chapters 2, 3
and 4 – revelation, natural theology and the Christological
approach to doctrine – are like three major road junctions.
They involve much more than a merely academic interest in
what a particular theologian has to say about them. What
we decide here in turn decides our whole approach not just

to theology but to Christian witness and to life in general. It is precisely the fact that Barth raises these questions in such a crucial way that makes him a key figure of our time.

Those who (like myself) cannot enjoy a book without knowing how it will end may be advised to turn first to the last chapter where I have drawn together my conclusions. But in each chapter and section I have tried to point out Barth's relevance, his strengths and weaknesses. From time to time I have tried to take bearings on the older, classical Protestant and Catholic positions in order to bring out points of contrast and also to try to see which comes closer to the truth. Above all I have tried to assess Barth's ideas in the light of the criterion which Barth himself insists is the ultimate criterion of all our ideas of God and man – Holy Scripture.

To those who want me to come clean and say where I stand I would simply repeat that there is much that we can learn from Barth. Just what these lessons are will, I hope, be made clear as the discussion proceeds. But on the debit side the main thrust of my criticisms is this, that for all his opposition to natural theology and his concern for being guided by Scripture, Barth is sometimes guilty of erecting a natural theology of his own. In a way Barth is too Christ-centred! This verdict might sound paradoxically odd for one Christian to pass upon another. But the more I read Barth, the stronger the impression grows that Barth's Christ is some-times very different from the Christ of the New Testament. To be more specific, Barth's central theme teaches that God does everything in and through Jesus Christ, through whom grace is all-triumphant. The essence of Barthianism is to re-shape all theology around this idea. It is precisely Barth's meticulous outworking of this *idea* of Christ that constitutes his strength and his weakness.

One further word of warning. Studies of Barth cannot be neatly pigeonholed into any one single department of theo-logy. Biography overlaps with the history of thought. Philos-ophy is mixed up with biblical theology. It could hardly be otherwise. For Christ touches the whole of reality and Barth is concerned above all with Christ. For those who want a more precise warning, the accent in chapter 1 falls on biography and the history of thought. Chapters 2 and 3 are concerned with revelation and natural theology, and are therefore studies partly in biblical theology and partly in philosophy. Chapter 4 deals with the biblical picture of Christ and is therefore largely a study in biblical theology and exegesis.

This study started life as an M.A. dissertation submitted in 1961 to the University of Nottingham with the title, *A Critical Examination of Karl Barth's Theological Method with Special Reference to his Doctrine of the Word of God.* But its shape and contents are now transformed almost beyond all recognition. A prototype version was delivered as the Tyndale Biblical Theology Lecture for 1963. Another version was read at the Puritan and Reformed Studies Conference at Westminster Chapel. But these likewise have undergone many changes in the intervening years. It remains for me to thank my many teachers and friends (not least the staff and readers of the Tyndale Press) for their helpful comments and criticisms.

1 THEOLOGICAL PILGRIMAGE

I BACKGROUND

Karl Barth was born on 10 May 1886. He grew up in a theological atmosphere. His father, Fritz Barth, taught at the Evangelical School of Preachers in Basel. When Karl was three, Barth senior took up the appointment of Professor of Church History and New Testament at Bern. As a student, Karl followed the normal German practice of doing the rounds at several universities. He began at Bern at the age of eighteen. He then moved to Berlin where he attended the lectures of the Old Testament scholar, Hermann Gunkel, and where he became a star pupil of the great liberal church historian, Adolf von Harnack. Not so long before, Harnack had published a series of popular lectures under the title, *Das Wesen des Christentums.*[1] They became at once something of a late-Victorian *Honest to God.*[2] Barth himself later described them as 'a notable peak' in the history of nineteenth-century theology.[3] According to Harnack, Christianity as we know it was largely the creation of the apostle Paul and the later church.[4] But the essential gospel has nothing

---

[1] Leipzig, 1900. Eng. tr. by T. B. Saunders, *What is Christianity? Sixteen Lectures Delivered in the University of Berlin during the Winter-Term 1899–1900* (Williams and Norgate, 1901). The work has been reprinted with an introduction by R. Bultmann (Stuttgart, 1950), Eng. tr., New York, 1957. References below are to the Eng. tr. of 1901.

[2] For a summary of the book and its impact see Stephen Neill, *The Interpretation of the New Testament, 1861–1961* (O.U.P., 1964), pp. 130–136.

[3] In a paper on 'Evangelical Theology in the Nineteenth Century' in *God, Grace and Gospel*, translated by J. S. McNab (*S.J.T. Occasional Papers No. 8*) (Oliver and Boyd, 1959), p. 57.

[4] *What is Christianity?*, pp. 175ff.

to do with the incarnation of a supernatural Word of God. Jesus was a man, the child of his age, who has found 'rest and peace for his soul, and is able to give life and strength to others'.[5] *The Gospel, as Jesus proclaimed it, has to do with the Father only and not with the Son.*[6] Harnack summed it up under three heads: *Firstly, the kingdom of God and its coming. Secondly, God the Father and the infinite value of the human soul. Thirdly, the higher righteousness and the commandment of love.*[7] The uniqueness of Jesus lies in the fact that he was a living embodiment of his message.[8] Like none other before or since, he practised what he preached. It was 'his vocation to communicate this knowledge of God to others by word and by deed – and with it the knowledge that men are God's children'.[9] Such was the apologetic of the greatest ecclesiastical historian at the dawn of the century. Such was the teaching which Barth learned at Berlin.

After Berlin, Barth spent another term at Bern before switching to Tübingen where among other things he studied the New Testament under the eminent conservative scholar Adolf Schlatter. Finally he spent three terms at Marburg under Jülicher, Heitmüller and the man whom Barth himself called '*the* theological teacher of my student days',[1] Wilhelm Herrmann.

Herrmann was the last of the impressive line of liberal dogmatic theologians which began with F. D. E. Schleiermacher (1768–1834) and continued through A. B. Ritschl (1822–89). Their writings were devoured by Barth and his generation. On the one hand, these theologians unanimously rejected the idea of the Bible as the Word of God written. On the other hand, they saw that theology could not be built upon the basis of abstract philosophical arguments. What they had in common was a desire to find some common denominator of religious experience which would be self-evident

---

[5] *Op. cit.*, p. 37.   [6] *Op. cit.*, p. 144 (italics Harnack's).
[7] *Op. cit.*, p. 51 (italics again Harnack's).
[8] *Op. cit.*, pp. 124–146.   [9] *Op. cit.*, p. 128.
[1] In 'The Principles of Dogmatics according to Wilhelm Herrmann' in *Theology and Church: Shorter Writings 1920–1928*, translated by Louise Pettibone Smith (S.C.M. Press, 1962), p. 238. For Barth's debt to Herrmann see this study.

to believer and unbeliever alike, and which could also serve as a yardstick to testing other religious ideas. Schleiermacher thought that he had found it in his belief that the essence of religion consists in a *sense of absolute dependence* upon God.[2] This led him to interpret sin as the clouding over of our consciousness of God, the desire to be free, when we should feel dependent.[3] And accordingly, Jesus was reinterpreted as a man who in everything had achieved perfect consciousness of God and who, in consequence, was able to pass on this gift to others.[4]

Ritschl's version of Christianity had a more ethical colouring. The key idea was the message of moral righteousness which Ritschl found in Jesus' preaching of the kingdom of God.[5] In a very real sense Jesus was the founder-member of the kingdom. He even gave his life out of loyalty to this vocation.[6]

Whereas Harnack stood in the tradition of Ritschl, Herrmann represented something of a return to Schleiermacher. All four accepted the methods and results of radical criticism. But they could equally have agreed with Herrmann that 'historical research cannot confront us with the Saviour Jesus Christ. It cannot help us to find the historical Christ whom Christians assert to be their salvation'.[7] The latter can only be done in *experience*. 'Out of what we *experience* in it, our faith in the Bible grows.'[8] Experience itself was his common denominator; it was also the yardstick which enabled Herrmann to reject such unwelcome doctrines as that of the inspiration of Scripture.[9]

---

[2] *The Christian Faith*, Eng. tr. based upon the 2nd German edition of 1830–31, edited by H. R. Mackintosh and J. S. Stewart (T. and T. Clark, Edinburgh, 1928, 1960), § 4, pp. 12ff. and *passim*.

[3] *Op. cit.*, §§ 65–78, pp. 269–325.   [4] *Op. cit.*, §§ 93–105, pp. 377–475.

[5] 'The conception we are in search of is given in the idea of the Christian community, which makes the Kingdom of God its task. This idea of the moral unification of the human race, through action prompted by universal love to our neighbour, represents a unity of many which belongs to the realm of the thoroughly defined, in other words, the good will.' *The Christian Doctrine of Justification and Reconciliation*, translated by H. R. Mackintosh and A. B. Macaulay (T. and T. Clark, Edinburgh, 1900), p. 280.

[6] *Op. cit.*, pp. 443–456.

[7] *Ethik* (1901), p. 109, quoted by Barth in *Theology and Church*, p. 250.

[8] Quoted by Barth, *op. cit.*, p. 252.   [9] *Cf.* Barth, *op. cit.*, pp. 252f.

The upshot of all this was that when Barth was ordained in 1908, his mind was steeped in nineteenth-century liberalism. It was a liberalism which was thoroughly at home with radical criticism and Idealist philosophy, and yet one which was marked by a deep streak of pietism and concern for practical Christian experience. For a time he was assistant editor of *Christliche Welt* (Christian World), and for two years he was an assistant pastor in Geneva. Then in 1911 came the appointment as pastor of Safenwil, a small agricultural and industrial town in Aargau on the German side of Switzerland. There now began a series of crises which were not only to transform Barth's thinking, but to change the course of theology in the twentieth century.

II BARTH THE DIALECTICAL THEOLOGIAN

The first crisis came with the outbreak of World War I, when ninety-three German intellectuals produced a manifesto supporting the Kaiser's war policy. 'Among them I found to my horror', Barth later wrote, 'the names of nearly all my theological teachers whom up to then I had religiously honoured. Disillusioned by their conduct, I perceived that I should not be able any longer to accept their ethics and dogmatics, their biblical exegesis, their interpretation of history, that at least for me the theology of the 19th century had no future.'[1]

But this crisis was in fact only a symptom of a slower, less spectacular, but nonetheless profound upheaval that was going on in Barth's mind as he went about his ministry. As week by week he was confronted with the problem of preaching and ministering to the needs of ordinary folk, he had become increasingly conscious of the shallowness and inadequacy of liberalism. Like Luther before him, he turned to the Bible for help and, in particular, to Paul's Epistle to the Romans. At the same time Barth was compulsively drawn to the writings of the Danish nineteenth-century philosopher, Søren Kierkegaard, and the Russian novelist, Fëodor Dostoievski. Here were men wrestling with life in a way scarcely dreamt of by the academic critic. There were

[1] *God, Grace and Gospel*, p. 58 (*S.J.T. Occasional Papers No. 8*), Eng. tr. by J. S. McNab (1959) of 'Gospel and Law', 'The Humanity of God' and 'Evangelical Theology in the 19th Century'.

also other influences. The religious socialism of the Swiss pastors, Leonhard Ragaz and Hermann Kutter, seemed to have a message for the times. And then there was his friend, Eduard Thurneysen, who was also making his own theological pilgrimage in the same direction as Barth.[2] All this bore tangible fruit not only in his thinking and preaching but in the publication of a commentary on Romans, *Der Römerbrief*, in 1919. Still not satisfied, Barth rewrote it and published a second, entirely different commentary on Romans in 1921.[3]

The Epistle to the Romans is one of the few works which really deserve the title 'epoch-making', even though the epoch in question was relatively short-lived. It is unlike every other commentary ever written on the subject. It is not devotional in any familiar sense. Nor yet is it critical. There is no introduction on authorship, date, background and contents. In his notes Barth largely dispenses with cross references and detailed explanations in the light of historical and philological research. In their place Barth has put together an enormous string of half-disconnected musings. Often they sit only very loosely to the text allegedly being expounded. But equally often they contain acute reflections on the ways of God and man. To read the book today is like suddenly being confronted with a Picasso after years of studying the old masters. But there was method in this apparent madness. Barth was convinced that, for all their learning, the critical commentators of his day had missed the point. Either they had got bogged down in a morass of technicalities.[4] Or they had tried to make the Bible say something different from what it actually did say.[5] In both cases they had failed to

[2] Between 1914 and 1925 Barth and Thurneysen kept up a lively correspondence. It reveals in a highly personal and very striking way what was going on in Barth's mind in these years. The English translation by James D. Smart is published under the title, *Revolutionary Theology in the Making: Barth–Thurneysen Correspondence, 1914–1925* (Epworth, 1964).

[3] *The Epistle to the Romans*, translated by Sir Edwyn C. Hoskyns (O.U.P., 1933, 1957[4]), is based on the 6th German edition which follows this 2nd edition. It is not to be confused with *A Shorter Commentary on Romans*, Eng. tr. by D. H. van Daalen (S.C.M. Press, 1959), which arose from lectures given early in the Second World War and which represents Barth's present position.

[4] *The Epistle to the Romans*, pp. 6ff.   [5] *Ibid.*

hear the Word of God. They had substituted the word of man for the Word of God.

The Epistle to the Romans was the finest flower of that exotic plant of the 1920s, Dialectical Theology. The movement sought to do justice to the Godness of God by describing Him as *Wholly Other*.[6] God was not an object existing in time and space. Following a Kantian line of thought, it was held that the infinite could not be grasped by the conceptual language of time and space. The latter was appropriate for finite things and people. But the infinite was not a matter of the finite scaled up. The infinite was by definition ineffable, utterly beyond the range of human words and thought. In other words, you could not say either what God was like or even what He was not like. Nevertheless, Scripture bore witness to the transcendent, inexpressible, infinite Word of God breaking into time and space in the person of Jesus Christ.[7] Scripture was not itself that revelation nor even a direct description of it. What it did was to describe its original impact upon humanity, and what it does today is to point the way to further encounter.

Dialectical Theology was no mere attempt to solve the philosophical puzzle of how the finite could become capable of receiving the infinite. It was also a theology of crisis or judgment.[8] The breaking in of the Word of God acts like a flare, brilliantly illuminating man's sinful, lost condition. It shows man as he is. It shows how man's religions and theologies are so often evasions, barriers erected by man to avoid real encounter with God. It shows that man knows nothing about God apart from God's revelation of Himself. In so doing, the Word also shows the way of reconciliation and salvation in Christ. And as it does this, it confronts man with the necessity of making a choice.

Thus in *The Epistle to the Romans* the characteristic themes of Barthian theology are already sounded: the sovereignty of God in face of the creation, the triumph of

---

[6] *Op. cit.*, p. 250; *cf.* p. 10; *God, Grace and Gospel*, pp. 35ff.; *cf.* T. F. Torrance, *Karl Barth: An Introduction to his Early Theology 1910–1931* (S.C.M. Press, 1962), pp. 48–95; H. Bouillard, *Karl Barth*, I, *Genèse et Évolution de la Théologie Dialectique* (Aubier, Paris, 1957).   [7] *Op. cit.*, p. 10.

[8] *Op. cit.*, p. 10. For the points mentioned in the following brief summary see, *e.g.*, pp. 35–54, 91–107, 149–164.

grace in the face of man's lostness in sin, and the fact that God's dealings with men are centred in Christ. Although Barth was later to modify and develop these themes in ways he could never have suspected at this time, the sovereign freedom of God, the triumph of grace and the centrality of Christ have remained the decisive factors in his teaching.

III THE PATH TO NEO-ORTHODOXY

A Roman Catholic theologian described Barth's commentary on Romans as a bomb falling on the playground of the theologians.[9] In the meantime, Barth hesitatingly accepted a call to teach theology in the University of Göttingen (1921). Again he was faced with a crisis. It was one thing to be a theological angry young man; it was another thing to teach theology. It was one thing to write a brilliant, impassioned, gesticulating book about the breaking in of the Word of God; it was something entirely different to hammer out a responsible account of Christian doctrine. It was at this point that Barth rediscovered the relevance of orthodoxy.

It happened almost by accident when Barth stumbled on the writings of the Post-Reformation Lutheran and Calvinistic theologians in the shape of the compends of Schmid and Heppe.[1] Liberalism had utterly failed to do justice to God's revelation of Himself in Christ. But when all was said and done, Dialectical Theology had only one doctrine – that of the encounter of the transcendent, inexpressible God with sinful man – and that was inadequately formulated.[2] As Barth pored over these works, he became aware of the range and depth of understanding of the writers of the more distant past. Admittedly, they did not speak on the wavelength of modern man. But they had a profounder grasp of the

[9] Karl Adam, 'Die Theologie der Krisis' in Hochland, 23rd year, II, 1926, 276f.
[1] Heinrich Schmid, Die Dogmatik der evangelisch-lutherischen Kirche (1843) was an anthology of Lutheran writings. The parallel volume of Calvinistic theology was H. Heppe, Die Dogmatik der evangelisch-reformierten Kirche (1861), new edition edited by E. Bizer (1935); Eng. tr. by G. T. Thomson, Reformed Dogmatics Set Out and Illustrated from the Sources (Allen and Unwin, 1950). In a foreword to this edition Barth tells of its impact on him.
[2] Barth himself has told of the later changes in his thinking in a paper on 'The Humanity of God' (1956), reprinted in God, Grace and Gospel, pp. 31–52. See especially pp. 34–37.

significance of revelation than any of the modern writers.
Barth came to see that the revelation contained in Scripture
spoke not only of judgment but of creation, not only of
grace but of covenant. Properly understood, it is relevant to
the whole range of human activity.

Barth also saw the inadequacy of the dialectical understanding of revelation. If God is really *Wholly Other*, then
nothing at all can be known or said about Him. At best we
can have inexpressible, mystical experiences. But we can
only say what led up to them and what we felt like after
them. We cannot describe the content of the revelation itself. There may be revelation, but *nothing* can be revealed.
For once we start talking about *things*, we are talking about
finite objects of this world and not about the *Wholly Other*
God. With his doctrine of sin and grace, Barth, the Dialectical Theologian, had really said more than his premises
allowed. If the *Wholly Other* really is *wholly other*, nothing
at all can be said about it. With their doctrine of the *Wholly
Other* God, the Dialectical Theologians had sawn off the
branch they were sitting on.

In retrospect, Barth realized how his quasi-philosophical
premises had distorted his view of revelation. He could even
speak of the 'strange incrustation of Kantian-Platonic conceptions' which encased his exposition of Romans.[3] He came
to see that revelation was not just a *pure act*,[4] and that God
was not simply *wholly other*. In point of fact, there were
two links missing from the early Barth's understanding of
revelation. One was a failure to appreciate the part Scripture played in revelation. The other was the doctrine of
analogy. We shall look at both more closely in the next
chapter. In the meantime, it is important to notice that it
was the orthodox writers of the past, not least Anselm of
Canterbury (on whom Barth wrote one of his most brilliant
books, *Fides Quaerens Intellectum* (1913)),[5] who helped Barth

[3] *Credo*, 1935; Eng. tr. by J. S. McNab (Hodder, 1936, 1964), p. 185.
[4] Even in *C.D.*, I, 1, pp. 44f. Barth describes the essence of revelation as a
pure act, but see below pp. 41–62, and *God, Grace and Gospel*, pp. 36f.
[5] Eng. tr. by Ian W. Robertson, *Anselm: Fides Quaerens Intellectum. Anselm's
Proof of the Existence of God in the Context of his Theological Scheme* (S.C.M. Press,
1960). On Barth's debt to Anselm, see pp. 11f., 29f. *C.D.*, II, 1, pp. 4, 92f.,
and T. F. Torrance, *op. cit.*, pp. 182ff., 193ff. See also below, pp. 47ff., 90ff.

towards a deeper, more biblical understanding of God's revelation of Himself.

But we have been jumping ahead. In 1925 Barth left Göttingen for Münster. He moved again, this time to Bonn, in 1930. Between 1923 and 1933 he edited, together with F. Gogarten, his lifelong friend E. Thurneysen and G. Merz, *Zwischen den Zeiten* (Between the Times), a journal which became the rallying-point of Dialectical Theology. Here Barth turned his mind to all manner of questions facing the contemporary church. Some of his articles and addresses were republished in book form. *The Word of God and the Word of Man* (1924)[6] ranges from the righteousness of God to the Christian's place in society. A similar anthology published four years later, *Theology and Church* (1928),[7] is weighted more with historical theology. But even here discussions of the church, culture and Roman Catholicism are to be found alongside of studies of Luther, Schleiermacher, Feuerbach and Herrmann. Barth also tried his hand again at writing commentaries. He wrote a commentary on 1 Corinthians 15 which was published under the title *The Resurrection of the Dead* (1924),[8] and *The Epistle to the Philippians* (1927).[9] In the early thirties Barth and Emil Brunner came to verbal blows on the subject of natural theology. In view of the fact that God was revealed in Christ Barth rejected it altogether. Brunner accused Barth of overstating his case. But of this we shall have more to say in chapter 3 where we shall subject their arguments to closer scrutiny.[1]

When Hitler came to power, Barth was teaching systematic theology at Bonn. He soon became 'the theological spearhead' of resistance.[2] He played a leading part in the

---

[6] Eng. tr. by Douglas Horton (Hodder, 1928).

[7] *Theology and Church: Shorter Writings 1920-1928*, Eng. tr. by Louise Pettibone Smith (S.C.M. Press, 1962).

[8] Eng. tr. by H. J. Stenning (Hodder and Stoughton, 1933).

[9] Eng. tr. by James W. Leitch (S.C.M. Press, 1962).

[1] See below, pp. 79-88.

[2] The phrase is E. H. Robertson's. It appears in his account of Barth's part in the Confessing Church in his *Christians against Hitler* (S.C.M. Press, 1962), p. 39. Barth's own writings on the struggle against the Nazis have been collected and published in the translation of P. T. A. Parker under the title *The German Church Conflict* (Lutterworth, 1965) (Ecumenical Studies in History No. 1). For a further account of the struggle and other literature see

founding of the Confessing Church and the framing of the Barmen Declaration of 1934 which simply and clearly professed allegiance to Christ in the face of Nazi oppression.[3] The Nazis lost little time in dismissing Barth from office. A Swiss subject, he left Germany and returned to his native Basel in 1935. He was almost at once appointed Professor of Theology at Basel, a chair he occupied until his retirement in April 1962.

The years at Basel were his glorious years. Students from all over the world flocked to attend his lectures and seminars, some of which were held in English as well as German.[4] He travelled abroad. He visited Scotland to deliver the 1937–1938 Gifford Lectures on natural theology at Aberdeen.[5] A steady stream of writings flowed from his pen. There was the course of lectures on the Apostles' Creed delivered just after the war amid the semi-ruins of the University of Bonn at the early hour of 7 a.m. These were published under the title *Dogmatics in Outline*,[6] and have gone through many

---

K. S. Latourette, *Christianity in a Revolutionary Age*, IV, *The Twentieth Century in Europe* (Eyre and Spottiswoode, 1962), pp. 257–269. Since the war Barth has been criticized for what some regard as an ambiguous attitude towards Communism. He visited Hungary in 1948 and became embroiled in a dispute by advising the Hungarian Christians that 'protest against . . . the communist system was not exactly the first and most urgent duty'. Rather, he told the Hungarian Christians to convert their fellow countrymen: 'Communism can be warded off only by a "better justice" on the part of the Western world' (both quotations from A. B. Come, *op. cit.*, p. 57, who puts the matter in perspective). See further the following for his stress on witness rather than political opposition and on the spiritual dangers of Western capitalism: *Die Kirche zwischen Ost und West*, 1949 and *Brief an einen Pfarrer in der Deutschen Demokratischen Republik*, 1958[2] (both publications of the Evangelischer Verlag, Zollikon-Zürich).

[3] Robertson gives an Eng. tr. in *op. cit.*, pp. 48–52.

[4] An account of Barth's teaching as given informally to students in the lecture room on a wide variety of topics is given by John D. Godsey in *Karl Barth's Table Talk* (Oliver and Boyd, 1963) (*S.J.T. Occasional Papers No. 10*).

[5] *The Knowledge of God and the Service of God According to the Teaching of the Reformation, Recalling the Scottish Confession of 1560*, Eng. tr. by J. L. M. Haire and Ian Henderson (Hodder and Stoughton, 1938, 1949[2]). Barth surmounted the problem created by the founder of the lectures, that they should deal with natural theology, by pointing out his lectures were devoted to a refutation of it by contrasting it with the Scottish Confession of 1560 (*cf.* pp. 3–12).

[6] Eng. tr. by G. T. Thomson (S.C.M. Press, 1949).

editions. A collection of Barth's shorter post-war writings was published under the title *Against the Stream*.[7] Immediately after his retirement Barth visited Chicago and Princeton where he gave a series of practical, semi-devotional lectures which were subsequently published as *Evangelical Theology: An Introduction*.[8] Among the most notable of Barth's works is his studies of the philosophers and theologians of the eighteenth and nineteenth centuries, *Die Protestantische Theologie im 19. Jahrhundert: Ihre Vorgeschichte und ihre Geschichte* (1947; 2nd edition, 1952). Unfortunately the English version, *From Rousseau to Ritschl*,[9] contains only eleven out of twenty-nine chapters of this massive, brilliantly penetrating, critical yet sympathetic study of the thinkers whom Barth rejects but who have conditioned the present theological ethos. At the other end of the theological scale *Deliverance to the Captives*[1] contains gospel sermons which Barth preached in Basel prison.

IV CHURCH DOGMATICS
Some of Barth's other writings will be mentioned later. Fuller bibliographies of Barthiana will be found in the works listed in the *Note on Books* at the end of this book.[2] When the last official count was made some time before his eightieth birthday the grand total amounted to 553 books, papers, sermons and articles.[3] This figure does not include new editions of old works, or translations into English, French, Dutch, Japanese, Czech, Hungarian and several other languages.

But the great work of Barth's life is his *Church Dogmatics*. This was actually begun in the 1920s, and first appeared as *Die Christliche Dogmatik im Entwurf* (Christian Dogmatics

---

[7] Eng. tr. by E. M. Delacour and S. Godman (S.C.M. Press, 1954).

[8] Eng. tr. by Grover Foley (Weidenfeld and Nicolson, 1963).

[9] Eng. tr. by Brian Cozens, revised by H. H. Hartwell and others (S.C.M. Press, 1959).

[1] Eng. tr. by M. Wieser (S.C.M. Press, 1961, 1966[2]).

[2] See below, pp. 154–159.

[3] A bibliography complete to the end of 1955 was compiled by Barth's secretary, Ch. von Kirschbaum. It appears in *Antwort*, pp. 945–960. This is supplemented by that compiled by Eberhard Busch in *Parrhesia*, pp. 709–723. This latter is complete up to January 1966.

in Outline) in 1927. But like the first version of the commentary on Romans, this was scrapped because its philosophical ideas still distorted what Barth really wanted to say about God's revelation of Himself.[4] The first volume proper appeared in 1932. Barth has been busy writing it ever since. And it is still incomplete.

This mammoth work now extends into some twelve volumes, each of some 400 to 900 pages. All twelve have been translated into English under the general editorship of G. W. Bromiley and T. F. Torrance, and are published by T. and T. Clark of Edinburgh. In actual fact, Barth himself calls each of these tomes *part-volumes* and even *half-part-volumes*! He reserves the word *volume* for the five major divisions into which the work falls. From now on, for the sake of convenience, *Church Dogmatics* will be abbreviated to *C.D.* when giving references. The volumes (in Barth's sense) will be indicated by Roman numerals, and the part-volumes by arabic numbers.

Volume I is entitled *The Doctrine of the Word of God. Prolegomena to Church Dogmatics.* It has two parts.[5] Its scope is to investigate the revelation witnessed to by the Bible.[6] It leads Barth to the doctrine of the Trinity, for revelation is none other than the revelation of the Father in the Son through the Holy Spirit.[7] God Himself is the ultimate principle of theology. In the course of this investigation Barth examines the part played by Scripture in revelation,[8] and also the way in which God reveals Himself through witness and preaching today.[9]

Volume II is also in two parts.[1] Having dealt with the underlying principles of theology, Barth now turns to *The*

---

[4] See Barth's own comments in his Foreword to *Church Dogmatics*, I, 1, pp. vii–xiv.

[5] *C.D.*, I, 1, Eng. tr. by G. T. Thomson (Edinburgh, 1936) (German original, 1932). *C.D.*, I, 2, Eng. tr. by G. T. Thomson and H. Knight (Edinburgh, 1956) (German original, 1938).

[6] *C.D.*, I, 1, pp. 1–335.

[7] *C.D.*, I, 1, pp. 339–560; *C.D.*, I, 2, pp. 1–454.

[8] *C.D.*, I, 2, pp. 457–740.   [9] *C.D.*, I, 2, pp. 743–884.

[1] *C.D.*, II, 1, Eng. tr. by T. H. L. Parker, W. B. Johnston, H. Knight and J. L. M. Haire (Edinburgh, 1957) (German original, 1940). *C.D.*, II, 2, Eng. tr. by G. W. Bromiley, J. C. Campbell, I. Wilson, J. S. McNab, H. Knight and R. A. Stewart (Edinburgh, 1957) (German original, 1942).

Doctrine of God. Here he is concerned with the nature and being of God, as Barth sees them revealed in Jesus Christ.[2] This leads on to a discussion of the attributes of God,[3] the way His nature is revealed in election[4] and the divine commandments.[5]

Volume III on *The Doctrine of Creation* is as long as the other two volumes put together! The first of its four parts[6] deals with the creation in the light of God's covenant with man. In so doing Barth gives his interpretation of the opening chapters of Genesis. The second part[7] deals with man in the whole range of his relationships with God and his fellow man. In Part 3[8] Barth sets out his teaching on providence,[9] evil,[1] and angels and demons.[2] Part 4[3] is devoted to a detailed examination of ethics, touching such questions as religious observances,[4] family and human relationships,[5] the state, capital punishment, war and the protection of life,[6] and vocation.[7]

Volume IV is entitled *The Doctrine of Reconciliation.*[8] After an initial survey of the subject,[9] Barth proceeds to discuss Christ's work as priest, king and prophet. This threefold way of approach goes back to Calvin. But whereas Calvin devoted only a few pages to the subject in his final Latin

---

[2] *C.D.*, II, 1, pp. 3–254.   [3] *C.D.*, II, 1, pp. 257–677.
[4] *C.D.*, II, 2, pp. 3–506.   [5] *C.D.*, II, 2, pp. 509–781.
[6] *C.D.*, III, 1, Eng. tr. by J. W. Edwards, O. Bussey and H. Knight (Edinburgh, 1958) (German original, 1945).
[7] *C.D.*, III, 2, Eng. tr. by H. Knight, G. W. Bromiley, J. K. S. Reid and R. H. Fuller (Edinburgh, 1960) (German original, 1948).
[8] *C.D.*, III, 3, Eng. tr. by G. W. Bromiley and R. J. Ehrlich (Edinburgh, 1961) (German original, 1950).
[9] *C.D.*, III, 3, pp. 3–288.   [1] *C.D.*, III, 3, pp. 289–368.
[2] *C.D.*, III, 3, pp. 369–531.
[3] *C.D.*, III, 4, Eng. tr. by A. T. Mackay, T. H. L. Parker, H. Knight, H. A. Kennedy and J. Marks (Edinburgh, 1961) (German original, 1951).
[4] *C.D.*, III, 4, pp. 3–115.   [5] *C.D.*, III, 4, pp. 116–323.
[6] *C.D.*, III, 4, pp. 324–564.   [7] *C.D.*, III, 4, pp. 565–685.
[8] *C.D.*, IV, 1, Eng. tr. by G. W. Bromiley (Edinburgh, 1956) (German original, 1953). *C.D.*, IV, 2, Eng. tr. by G. W. Bromiley (Edinburgh, 1958) (German original, 1955). *C.D.*, IV, 3, First Half, Eng. tr. by G. W. Bromiley (Edinburgh, 1961) (German original, 1959). *C.D.*, IV, 3, Second Half, Eng. tr. by G. W. Bromiley (Edinburgh, 1962) (German original, 1959).
[9] *C.D.*, IV, 1, pp. 3–154.

version of the *Institutes*,[1] Barth takes the three offices in turn and uses each as a vantage point from which to survey the whole panorama of Christ's reconciling work. Thus in Part 1 he looks at Christ as priest or servant. In so doing, he looks first at His obedience,[2] and then at the sin which this obedience counteracts.[3] After discussing the atoning work of the cross,[4] Barth finally turns to the benefits of Christ's priestly work for man[5] and the work of the Holy Spirit in applying it to him.[6]

Parts 2 and 3 of Volume IV follow the same symmetrical pattern. Part 2 deals with Christ's kingly work and man's sanctification, and Part 3 Christ's prophetic work. In each of these the place of the church is considered in relation to Christ's work,[7] but as yet there is no full treatment of the sacraments.[8] A Fourth Part was in preparation, but we understand that it will not now be completed.[9]

It has to be admitted that Barth's *Church Dogmatics* is not always easy going even for the initiated. Barth's liberal use of his own technical jargon and his way of putting things often sounds foreign in more ways than one. As the years have gone by, Barth does not seem to have grown any less long-winded. One side-effect of all this is that a cursory look at his chapter headings and their contents is apt to be more mystifying than revealing. But when all is said and done – and in the course of the following pages there will be occasion to raise damning objections to certain important aspects of Barth's teaching – Barth's *Church Dogmatics* is the most impressive theological work of modern times.

[1] *Institutes of the Christian Religion* (1559), II, xv.
[2] *C.D.*, IV, 1, pp. 157–357.   [3] *C.D.*, IV, 1, pp. 358–513.
[4] *C.D.*, IV, 1, pp. 514–642.
[5] *C.D.*, IV, 1, pp. 643–739.   [6] *C.D.*, IV, 1, pp. 740–779.
[7] *Cf. C.D.*, IV, 1, pp. 643–739 with *C.D.*, IV, 2, pp. 614–726 and *C.D.*, IV, 3, 2, pp. 681–901.
[8] Barth has come down on the side of believers' baptism in a slight essay on *The Teaching of the Church regarding Baptism*, Eng. tr. by E. A. Payne (S.C.M. Press, 1948, 1956[4]).
[9] The British publishers regretfully report that the author has also decided not to undertake a projected Volume V on *eschatology*, a term which Barth uses in the sense of Romans 8:23; Luke 21:28; Ephesians 4:30; Hebrews 11:35 (*cf. C.D.*, i, 1, p. 469). This would have treated the full completion of the Christian hope.

Before we turn to look at some of his key ideas, it is worth while making one further observation. Despite its breath-taking scale and vast erudition, the *Church Dogmatics* is not an encyclopaedia of religion and ethics. It is, in fact, con-structed like a monster sandwich with practical application alternating with layers of detailed critical exegesis of Scrip-ture and the great thinkers of the past and present. The former – Barth's preaching – is printed in large type. The latter appears in small type. In some ways the former is the more important; the latter is more the raw material of which the preaching is the finished product. It could be said of Barth what was said of 'Rabbi' Duncan, that his applica-tion is all doctrine, and his doctrine is all application. The point could be pressed even further by saying that his doc-trine is all apologetics, and his apologetics is all doctrine. For from first to last knowledge of God is not something separate from the gospel. It is not an object which man can possess or dispose of at will. It is not something that man can arrive at by subtle arguments and philosophical proofs. From beginning to end knowledge of God is a gift of God to be received by faith in humble obedience.

> The knowledge of God occurs in the fulfilment of the revelation of His Word by the Holy Spirit, and therefore in the reality and with the necessity of faith and its obedi-ence. Its content is the existence of Him whom we must fear above all things because we may love Him above all things; who remains a mystery to us because He Himself has made Himself so clear and certain to us.[1]

In making this point, Barth is reiterating a truth re-peatedly taught by Jesus and the New Testament writers. 'All things have been delivered to me by my Father; and no one knows the Son except the Father, and no one knows the Father except the Son and any one to whom the Son chooses

---

[1] *C.D.*, II, 1, p. 3. The theme recurs throughout Barth's writings. It is developed at length in *C.D.*, I, 1, pp. 141–283; *C.D.*, II, 1, pp. 3–254; and more briefly in *Dogmatics in Outline*, pp. 15–49; and *Evangelical Theology*, pp. 15–59, 96–105, 159–170.

to reveal him.'[2] Jesus Himself is the way, the truth and the life; no-one comes to the Father, but by Him.[3] Christian theology is the study of this truth in its depth, implications and applications.[4]

[2] Matthew 11:27; cf. 7:21–27; 13:10–23; Mark 4:1–20; Luke 8:4–15; John 1:12f.; 3:3ff.; 5:20ff.; 8:12; 12:39ff.; 16:13f.; 17:6ff.; Acts 28:25ff.; Romans 11:33ff.; 1 Corinthians 1:18–2:5; 2 Corinthians 3:14–4:6; Galatians 1:15; Ephesians 1:9–2:8; 2 Peter 1:21; cf. also Isaiah 6:9f.

[3] John 14:6.

[4] In the broadest sense of the term, *theology* is simply thinking and speaking about God and his ways with men (*C.D.*, I, 1, p. 1). But if it is to be true, it must correspond with the reality it purports to speak about. Hence, there arises the need for *dogmatics*, or 'the science in which the Church, in accordance with the state of its knowledge at different times, takes account of the content of its proclamation critically, that is, by the standard of Holy Scripture and under the guidance of its Confessions' (*Dogmatics in Outline*, p. 9; cf. *C.D.*, I, 1, pp. 11ff.). It is a science in this sense that: '1. Like all other so-called sciences, it is a human effort after a definite object of knowledge. 2. Like all other sciences, it follows a definite, self-consistent path of knowledge. 3. Like all other sciences, it is in a position of being accountable for this path to itself and to every one – everyone who is capable of effort after this object and therefore of following this path' (*C.D.*, I, 1, p. 7). But this means that dogmatics is concerned with revelation, and in the nature of the case it must be pursued in faith. Dogmatics might well be defined as faith taking stock of itself for the benefit of the church; and apologetics as faith taking stock of itself for the benefit of the world. Barth examines the nature and various branches of theology in *C.D.*, I, 1, pp. 1–47, 284–335; *Dogmatics in Outline*, pp. 9–14; *Evangelical Theology: An Introduction* (1963); and *Anselm: Fides Quaerens Intellectum* (1960). As the latter title indicates, theology is a matter of faith seeking understanding. The book itself is a reinterpretation of Anselm's ontological argument, showing that it essentially follows Anselm's dictum: *Credo ut intelligam* (I believe in order that I may understand). On this work see further below, pp. 90ff.

2 THE WORD OF GOD AND THE KNOWLEDGE OF GOD

The central question of religion today is: How do we know God? Barth came to his answer only after a difficult, uphill, theological pilgrimage. And even then he still had to spend long years revising, correcting and amplifying his first thoughts. We know God, Barth says, only as He is pleased to reveal Himself in His Word. This Word, he adds, comes to us today through the Scriptures and in the power of the Holy Spirit. It is the action of God's free grace.

In this chapter we shall look at this answer from three angles. First (under the heading I *The Word of God in its Threefold Form*) we shall ask what Barth means when he speaks of the Word of God. Secondly (under the heading II *Revelation and the Bible*) we shall investigate the connection between the Word of God in Christ and God's Word as it is written in the Bible. Finally (under the heading III *The Word of God and the Doctrine of the Trinity*) we shall consider how Barth's view of revelation leads to the doctrine of the Trinity.

I THE WORD OF GOD IN ITS THREEFOLD FORM
In the *Church Dogmatics* Barth begins his account of the Word of God by describing what he calls its *threefold form*.[1] By this he means the Word of God in preaching, the Word of God in Scripture and Jesus Christ as the Word of God. Perhaps his meaning will become clearer if we invert Barth's order and look at the last first.

a. Jesus Christ the Word of God
The *primary form*[2] of the Word of God is Jesus Christ Him-

---

[1] *C.D.*, I, 1, pp. 98–140. [2] *C.D.*, I, 1, p. 135.

self. In the strictest sense of the term He is the Word of God, the revelation of God. In speaking this way, Barth is adopting the language of John 1 : 1, 14; Revelation 19 : 13 (*cf.* Hebrews 1 : 2). But he is doing more than this. He is drawing attention to the fact that Jesus is the unique mediator of revelation, no less than of salvation. Indeed, there is a sense in which the two are really different ways of looking at the same thing. Salvation can be regarded as a change of status, the gift of new life, being rescued from sin and its consequences.[3] Or it can be expressed in terms of a new knowledge of God.[4] In both cases it is the same work of the same Jesus Christ, as is shown by Matthew 11 : 27ff., Luke 19 : 9, John 14 : 6–10, 1 Corinthians 1 : 30 and the passages mentioned here below and on p. 29, n. 2.

Barth himself puts it like this:

> Revelation in fact does not differ from the Person of Jesus Christ, and again does not differ from the reconciliation that took place in Him. To say revelation is to say, 'The Word became flesh.'[5]

It would not be too much to say that this is the pivot of all Barth's thinking. In the pages that follow we shall try to see how he develops this thought not only with regard to revelation, but also how it becomes the starting-point for all his teaching. We shall also have cause to ask whether this Christocentric approach does not lead Barth to overstate the biblical case by making all revelation *saving* revelation,[6] as this passage of Barth's might be taken to imply. But for the present it is sufficient to note that Barth has put his finger upon a key biblical theme: Christ is the unique mediator of

---

[3] *Cf.* (*e.g.*) Matthew 26:28; Mark 10:45; John 1:12f.; 5:24; 6:35; 7:37ff.; Acts 4:12; Romans 5:9ff.; 2 Corinthians 5:18–21; Ephesians 1:3–2:22; 3:14–19; Colossians 1:19f. On the subject of salvation see E. M. B. Green, *The Meaning of Salvation* (Hodder and Stoughton, 1965).

[4] *Cf.* (*e.g.*) Matthew 11:27–30; John 17:3, 6ff., 25f.; 2 Corinthians 4:6; Ephesians 1:9.

[5] *C.D.*, I, 1, p. 134.

[6] It is one thing for light to shine in the darkness; it is another for the darkness to receive it, as John 1:5 and the contexts of the passages mentioned dealing with salvation make clear. On Barth's universalism see below, pp. 130–133.

revelation, no less than of salvation. In revelation we are concerned with God Himself in Christ.

b. Scripture as the Word of God

The *second form* of the Word of God is Holy Scripture.[7] Barth sees Scripture as the *witness of the prophets and apostles* (by which he means the biblical writers generally). The Old Testament writers look forward to Christ; the New Testament writers look back to Him.

In one sense, therefore, revelation is quite different from Scripture – just as Jesus was quite different from His disciples. And yet there is a sense in which the two coincide,[8] as G. W. Bromiley, joint-editor of the English edition of the *Church Dogmatics*, explains: 'The word "witness" is a dangerous one if used in its ordinary sense, but if we think of the Bible as a witness in the way in which the Bible itself describes the prophets and apostles as witnesses – "he that receiveth you, receiveth me" – it is perhaps not quite so objectionable as some critics of Barth suppose. This is at least how Barth himself is thinking of it, and in this sense it has the merit of being a word which the Bible uses even about itself (*cf.* John 5 : 39).'[9]

From one point of view, the Bible is not the Word of God. It is the word of man. As a book, it is just a mass of paper printed with ink. But it becomes God's Word in the event of revelation. Revelation is no static thing but encounter with the living God. Or to quote Barth:

> The Bible is God's Word so far as God lets it be His Word, so far as God speaks through it . . . The Bible therefore *becomes* God's Word in this event, and it is to its *being* in this *becoming* that the tiny word 'is' relates, in the statement that the Bible *is* God's Word.[1]

But the Bible is also unique in view of the unique relationship in which the biblical writers stand to Jesus Christ:

---

[7] *C.D.*, I, 1, pp. 111–124; *cf. C.D.*, I, 2, pp. 457–537.

[8] *C.D.*, I, 1, pp. 127f.

[9] In *Karl Barth's Doctrine of Inspiration*, a paper read at the 929th Ordinary General Meeting of the Victoria Institute, 18 April 1955, p. 69. *Cf.* Matthew 10:40; Luke 10:16; John 13:20. *Cf.* also *C.D.*, I, 2, pp. 487ff.

[1] *C.D.*, I, 1, pp. 123f.; *cf. C.D.*, I, 2, p. 457.

We cannot speak about Yahweh's covenant with Israel without at once speaking of Moses and the prophets. Similarly in the New Testament, indissolubly bound up with Jesus Christ, there are the figures of His disciples, His followers, His apostles, those who are called by Him, the witnesses of His resurrection, those to whom He Himself has directly promised and given His Holy Spirit. The Church can say anything at all about the event of God and man only because something unique has taken place between God and these specific men, and because in what they wrote, or what has been written by them, they confront us as living documents of that unique event. To try to ignore them is to ignore that unique event. The existence of these specific men is the existence of Jesus Christ for us and for all men. It is in this function that they are distinguished from us and from all other men, whom they resemble in everything else. Therefore the specific and explicit self-witness of Scripture consists in the fact that, from the standpoint of the form in which its content is offered and alone offered to us, it is the witness of the existence of these specific men.[2]

In other words, if we want to know anything at all about Christ, we must approach Him through the witnesses that He Himself has specially commissioned.[3] There is no way of short-circuiting them and getting a direct vision of God.

All this raises a number of very basic questions. But it will help to clarify Barth's position if we postpone discussion of them until we have taken a look at what Barth calls the *third form* of the Word of God.

c. Preaching as the Word of God
The *third form* of the Word of God is *preaching* or

---

[2] *C.D.*, I, 2, p. 486.
[3] Barth bases his view upon his exegesis of the following passages: Mark 3:14; Matthew 10:19f., 40; 16:18f.; 18:18; 28:20; Luke 10:16; John 14:26; 16:13; 17:8, 20; 20:21, 23; Acts 1:8; 2:1f.; 1:2f.; 3:4f.; 2 Corinthians 5:18, 20; Galatians 1:1, 15 (*cf.* Jeremiah 1:5); Ephesians 4:11 (*cf. C.D.*, I, 2, pp. 487f.). He follows the New Testament writers in interpreting the Old Testament Christologically; *cf.* Matthew 5:17; Luke 4:21; 18:31; 24:13f., 44; John 1:45; 5:39, 46; 10:35; Acts 17:11; 18:24f.; 26:22; Romans 1:2; 3:21; 4:23f.; 9:17; 15:4; 16:26; 1 Corinthians 9:10; 10:11; 15:3; Hebrews 10:7; 2 Peter 1:19 (*cf. C.D.*, I, 2, pp. 488ff.). See also below, pp. 64f., 70f., 100ff.

proclamation.[4] When Barth speaks in this way he has in mind not merely the formal Sunday sermon from the pulpit but all kinds of Christian witness. It may be the Sunday school lesson; it may be a theological treatise. It may be a personal word of testimony; it may be a Bible story told to children by their mother at bedtime. The point is that Barth is trying to see the relationship between the Word of God here, the Word of God as it is in Scripture and Jesus Christ.

Barth sees this relationship as sacramental.[5] His comparison is a good one. Just as the bread and wine in the Lord's Supper remain bread and wine, but become vehicles of communion; so the human words of Christian witness are not transubstantiated into something else, but become the means through which God speaks to men today, even though they remain human words.

But this raises the crucial question: How do we know that this witness is true? Barth's reply is that our witness must rest ultimately upon divine commissioning,[6] that the power of our witness rests ultimately with God and not with ourselves,[7] that we can only proceed to witness in an attitude of humble prayerfulness,[8] and that the truth of all witnessing must be tested by comparing it with Scripture.

This last point rests upon Barth's view of Scripture as the normative testimony of the specially commissioned witnesses which we have already described. It remains to be stressed that all three forms are inter-related, and that in practice we do not have one without the other two:

> The *revealed Word of God* we know only from the Scripture adopted by Church proclamation, or from Church proclamation based on Scripture.
> The *written Word of God* we know only through the revelation which makes proclamation possible, or through the proclamation made possible by revelation.
> The *proclaimed Word of God* we know only by knowing

[4] *C.D.*, I, 1, pp. 98–111.
[5] *C.D.*, I, 1, p. 98; *cf.* Calvin, *Institutes of the Christian Religion*, IV, xiv, 18; and *The Second Helvetic Confession* of 1566, composed by H. Bullinger, Art. 19, 8: '*Nam Verbo Dei fiunt, quae antea non fuerunt, sacramenta. Consecrantur enim Verbo et sanctificata esse ostenduntur ab eo, qui instituit.*'
[6] *C.D.*, I, 1, pp. 99ff.   [7] *C.D.*, I, 1, pp. 101ff.
[8] *C.D.*, I, 1, pp. 110f.; *cf. Evangelical Theology: An Introduction*, pp. 159–170.

the revelation attested through Scripture, or by knowing
the Scripture which attests revelation.[9]

In all three forms it is God in Christ graciously taking the
initiative and encountering man. The point may be put even
more strongly by saying that for Barth *all God's dealings
with men are effected in and through the person of Jesus
Christ.* This would seem to be the basic axiom underlying
Barth's entire exposition of the Word of God.[1] Christ may
well come to us mediated or *veiled*[2] in human words. But if
we have any knowledge of God at all, it is knowledge of God
through Christ.

II REVELATION AND THE BIBLE

We now turn to some of the questions raised by Barth's
view of the Word of God. The scope of this study requires
us to be highly selective.[3] We shall therefore confine ourselves to three of the burning issues raised by Barth's views.
And we shall put each in the form of a question. In so
doing we shall not attempt to work out a complete doctrine
of the inspiration and authority of the Bible. Our aim is the
much more modest one of asking whether what Barth has to
say is relevant to the contemporary debates on the subject.

a. How do we know that the Bible is the Word of God?

In answering this question, Barth gives the same answer that
Calvin and the Reformers gave. We may (with Barth) sum

---

[9] *C.D.*, I, 1, p. 136.
[1] See especially above, pp. 19f., 28f., 32, and below, pp. 78ff., 99ff.
[2] 'The facts are that *God Himself veils Himself and in the very process . . . unveils
Himself*' (*C.D.*, I, 1, p. 192; *cf. ibid.*, pp. 184–212).
[3] See, in particular, for more detailed studies of Barth's view of revelation,
Gordon H. Clark, *Karl Barth's Theological Method* (Presbyterian and Reformed
Publishing Co., Philadelphia, 1963); P. Courthial, 'La Conception
barthienne de l'Ecriture Sainte examinée du point de vue réforme' in *La
Revue Réformée*, No. 66, 1966/2, Vol. XVII, pp. 1–35; and the important,
detailed study of Klaas Runia, *Karl Barth's Doctrine of Holy Scripture* (Eerdmans, Grand Rapids, 1962). All the standard works on Barth deal with this
question. For a more Barthian appreciation of Barth, as compared with
Brunner and the teaching of the great Protestant and Catholic theologians
since the Reformation, see J. K. S. Reid, *The Authority of Scripture. A Study of
the Reformation and Post-Reformation Understanding of the Bible* (Methuen, 1957).

it up in Calvin's words: 'The highest proof of Scripture derives in general from the fact that God in person speaks in it.'[4]

We might admire the Bible as a fine piece of literature. We might value it as a remarkable source-book for the history of the ancient world. We might be impressed with the way in which modern archaeology has confirmed so much of its reporting of places and incidents. But when all such factors are put together, they do not add up to making the Bible the Word of God. They may indicate a very remarkable collection of documents. Something more is needed if we are to be convinced that the Bible is the Word of God.

Such evidence can only come from two quarters. On the one hand, there are the Bible's own claims about itself.[5] But it is one thing to make a claim; it is something else to make that claim good. And so we are brought back to the other line of evidence, the Bible's power to authenticate itself as the Word of God.

It may be objected that this is a vicious circle. In reply we may with Barth point out that the argument is circular, but not viciously so.

We have to admit to ourselves and to all who ask us about this question that the statement that the Bible is the Word of God is an analytical statement, a statement which is grounded only in its repetition, description and interpretation, and not in its derivation from any major propositions. It must either be understood as grounded in itself and preceding all other statements or it cannot be understood at all. The Bible must be known as the Word of *God* if it is to be *known* as the Word of God. The doctrine of Holy Scripture in the Evangelical Church is that this logical circle is the circle of self-asserting, self-attesting truth into which it is equally impossible to enter as it is to emerge from it: the circle of our freedom which as such is also the circle of our captivity.[6]

---

[4] Calvin, *Institutes of the Christian Religion*, I, vii, 4 (the version quoted here is that of Ford Lewis Battles, Library of Christian Classics, Vol. XX (S.C.M. Press, 1961), p. 78); *cf.* Barth, *C.D.*, I, 1, p. 128 (which also gives details of other theologians).

[5] On this, see below, pp. 54–62; *cf.* above, pp. 32f.   [6] *C.D.*, I, 2, p. 535.

By the very nature of the case, 'objective' proof is as impossible as it is irrelevant. For there is no independent vantage point from which we can look at God and then at the Bible, and then make an appraisal of the latter.[7] To descend to a crude analogy (even though it originated with Calvin)[8]: the Scriptures are like glasses which bring the truth about God and man into focus. If we take them off, all we get are dim and confused impressions. The value of the spectacles can be seen only by using them. So it is with the Bible. It contains its own authentication.

To use another analogy, recognizing the Bible as the Word of God is like recognizing colours. How do we know that this object is yellow? We might say that it is like other yellow things. But how do we know that they are yellow? In the last analysis, we know yellowness by seeing it. It cannot be described in terms other than itself. It cannot be reduced to anything else. It is self-evident. When we see it and grasp it, we know it.

The ultimate truth of revelation is self-evident. On the level of historical and other facts, the biblical writings are (in principle at least) verifiable and falsifiable like any other historical document. We can do this by checking their assertions against what is known from other sources. This is the job of the biblical historian and archaeologist. But when we come to statements in the Bible about what God is like and what are His relationships with man, we have no such way of checking, apart from the statements themselves. In the last analysis, the truth of the Bible on this level is on the same level as knowing Christ. The Bible has much to say both about itself and about Christ, but the truth of these claims can ultimately be verified only in experience. 'Ask, and it will be given you; seek, and you will find; knock, and it will be opened to you.'[9] 'If any man's will is to do his will, he shall know whether the teaching is from God or whether I am speaking on my own authority.'[1]

[7] This point depends, of course, upon the impossibility of a valid natural theology. On this, see below, pp. 77–98.
[8] *Institutes of the Christian Religion*, I, xiv, 1.
[9] Luke 11:9; Matthew 7:7.
[1] John 7:17.

In describing the truth of revelation as self-evident one further proviso has to be made. Neither Barth, nor Calvin, nor the Bible regards it as a sort of knock-down argument which will win the acknowledgment of all and sundry. It is perfectly possible to read the words of Scripture and see only the words of men. 'The unspiritual man does not receive the gifts of the Spirit of God, for they are folly to him, and he is not able to understand them because they are spiritually discerned.'[2] Men need to be born again of the Spirit before they can see the kingdom of God.[3] In the last analysis, revelation of the Word of God takes place when and where it pleases God in His loving wisdom.[4] But when it does, it comes with authority and power.

b. Why the Bible in particular?

The question might well be asked: Why is the Bible normative for our understanding of the Word of God? Why these particular Scriptures and not others? Why the Epistles of Paul and John and not those of Clement of Rome and Ignatius of Antioch? These questions are made acute by the fact that the latter were written not much later than the last of the biblical writings (and on some critical theories, even earlier). The uncanonical 1 Clement might well have been written prior to or about the same time as the canonical Revelation to John. In other words, chronologically both stand pretty well equally close to the historical Jesus.[5] These questions are rendered doubly acute by Barth's justified recognition that God also speaks through non-canonical speakers and writers.[6]

---

[2] 1 Corinthians 2:14.   [3] John 3:3, 5; cf. 1:12f.
[4] See above, pp. 28f., and below, pp. 51–66. Cf. Calvin, Institutes of the Christian Religion, II, ii, 20; III, xxi, 1. On revelation in nature see below, pp. 94–98.
[5] Although there has never been any really serious doubt as to the relative value of the two books some weight to this question is given by the fact that an important biblical manuscript like the fifth-century Codex Alexandrinus contains 1 and 2 Clement alongside of the canonical scriptures, and some Eastern churches were dubious about the canonicity of the Apocalypse (on this latter point see R. H. Charles, The Revelation of St. John, I.C.C., I, 1920, pp. xcvii–ciii).
[6] If God spoke only through the canonical scriptures, there would be no point in speaking, preaching and writing about God. The only way of witnessing

Barth's reply to these questions has already been antici-
pated in the foregoing discussion. It is, in fact, two-pronged.[7]
On the one hand, he points to the self-authenticating
character of Scripture.[8] On the other, he appeals to the
special position of the writers of Scripture as the specially
commissioned witnesses[9] of his original revelation. It is
these two factors which distinguish the Scriptures from all
other writings.

> The Word of God is God Himself in Holy Scripture. For
> God once spoke as Lord to Moses and the prophets, to the
> Evangelists and apostles. And now through their written
> word He speaks as the same Lord to His Church. Scripture
> is holy and the Word of God, because by the Holy Spirit
> it became and will become to the Church a witness to
> divine revelation.[1]

There is no need to retrace our steps over this ground, but
one further point is worth noting. It concerns the fact that
when the church recognized the canon of Scripture it was
not a case of the church bestowing its authority upon Scripture, but of recognizing an authority that was already there.

> When we adopt the Canon of the Church we do not say
> that the Church itself, but that the revelation which
> underlies and controls the Church, attests these witnesses
> and not others as the witnesses of revelation and therefore
> as canonical for the Church.[2]

This line of thought cuts clean across a good deal of
catholic and ecumenical thinking which seeks to blur the
distinction between the authority of the Scriptures and the
authority of the church,[3] or even to set the latter above the
former. But in making this point, Barth has history on his

---

would be to read out or display passages of Scripture, or to thrust copies of
the Bible at people.

[7] For Barth's views on the canon see especially *C.D.*, I, 1, pp. 113–124; *C.D.*,
I, 2, pp. 473–485. *Cf.* also *C.D.*, II, 2, pp. 480–506 for Barth's views of the
place of *tradition*.

[8] See above, pp. 35–38.   [9] See above, pp. 32f.

[1] *C.D.*, I, 2, p. 457.   [2] *C.D.*, I, 2, p. 474.

[3] An example of this way of thinking appears in the statement on 'Scripture
and Tradition' in *Conversations between the Church of England and the Methodist
Church. A Report to the Archbishops of Canterbury and York and the Conference of the*

side. There has never been a general council, recognized by
the whole church, which rubber-stamped its authority upon
the canon of Scripture. The earliest known list to give the
full number of books of the present New Testament canon
appears in the Easter Letter of Athanasius, written in AD
367, to guard his flock against heretics and their pseudo-
Scriptures.[4] What, wrote Athanasius, distinguishes the Scriptures from other writings (however valuable) are the facts
that the Scriptures are 'God-inspired' ($\theta\epsilon\acute{o}\pi\nu\epsilon\upsilon\sigma\tau os$) in
a way which other writings are not, and that they have been
handed down 'by those who were eye-witnesses . . . of the
word from the beginning'. The first council officially to recog-
nize our full canon was the local one at Hippo (AD 393),
closely followed by one at Carthage (AD 397).[5] But, in point
of fact, the canonicity of the New Testament writings was
substantially recognized long before that.[6] In short, recog-

---

Methodist Church (Church Information Office and the Epworth Press, 1963),
pp. 15–19. The report admits that tradition 'gives no answer to the problem
acutely raised in many critical periods of Church history, how to diagnose
virus, poison in the blood stream, and what are the remedies and safeguards
against it' (p. 18). On the other hand, it claims: 'Now we are coming to see
that scripture and tradition ought not to be put over against one another.
Both are gifts and instruments of the Holy Spirit within the Church. Behind
both is the Living Word of God, the Word made flesh in Jesus Christ, the
Word who speaks now through the whole life of the Church, its thought and
worship, its life and behaviour, the whole manifold and varied existence of
the only Holy Catholic Church . . . The Scriptures are also part of the tradition
itself, written as they were in the Church, by the Church, for the Church' (pp.
17f.). This view was rightly repudiated by the minority report (*ibid.*, pp. 57f.).
Cf. also the debate between Oscar Cullmann and the Roman Catholic theologian J. R. Geiselmann in *Christianity Divided: Protestant and Roman Catholic
Theological Issues*, edited by D. J. Callahan, H. A. Obermann, D. J. O'Hanlon
(Sheed and Ward, 1962), pp. 3–72.
[4] Greek text and Eng. tr. in A. Souter, *The Text and Canon of the New Testament*,
revised edition by C. S. C. Williams (Duckworth, 1954), pp. 196–200.
[5] On the utterances and historicity of conciliar pronouncements see Souter,
op. cit., pp. 178ff.
[6] 'Its kernel, the Four Gospels and the 13 Epistles by St. Paul, had come to
be accepted *c.* 130 and were placed on the same footing with the O.T.
between 170 and 220 . . . Doubts persisted, esp. in the case of Heb., Jude, 2
Pet., 2 and 3 Jn. and Rev., as is shown, e.g., by a list drawn up by Eusebius'
The Oxford Dictionary of the Christian Church, edited by F. L. Cross (O.U.P.,
1957), p. 229. On Eusebius (*c.* 265–339), *Ecclesiastical History*, III, 25, see
Souter, *op. cit.*, pp. 170f.

nition of the canon of Scripture was not an official act of the church but a growing awareness of the intrinsic authority of the Scriptures.

But Barth has not only early church history on his side. His view of authority reflects that of Mark 7 : 1–13, where Jesus condemns those who substitute religious tradition for the Scriptures, 'thus making void the word of God through your tradition which you hand on'.[7]

c. What is the connection between encounter with God and revealed truth?

In modern times there has grown up a habit among theologians of treating revelation as personal encounter with God and then of playing it off against the idea of revealed truth.[8] William Temple did so when he wrote: 'There is no such thing as revealed truth. There are truths of revelation, that is to say, propositions which express the results of correct thinking concerning revelation; but they are not themselves directly revealed.'[9] There is a good deal in Barth to suggest that he might be following suit. And there is no lack of commentators on Barth who have taken him in this way,[1] particularly in view of the sharp line Barth draws

[7] Mark 7:13; *cf.* 7:6f. with Isaiah 29:13.

On this see J. I. Packer, 'Contemporary Views of Revelation' in *Revelation and the Bible: Contemporary Evangelical Thought*, edited by Carl F. Henry (Tyndale Press, 1959), pp. 87–104; Daniel Day Williams, *Interpreting Theology, 1918–1952* (S.C.M. Press, 1953), pp. 40–67; John Baillie, *The Idea of Revelation in Recent Thought* (O.U.P., 1956), pp. 19–61; H. D. McDonald, *Theories of Revelation: An Historical Study, 1860–1960* (Allen and Unwin, 1963), pp. 16off.

[9] *Nature, Man and God. Being the Gifford Lectures Delivered in the University of Glasgow in the Academical Years 1932–1933 and 1933–1934* (Macmillan, 1934, 1953), p. 317.

[1] On this see H. D. McDonald, *op. cit.*, p. 169, and *Ideas of Revelation: An Historical Study A.D. 1700 to A.D. 1800* (Macmillan, 1959), p. 73, n. 1; J. Hamer, *Karl Barth. L'Occasionalisme Théologique de Karl Barth. Étude sur sa Méthode* (Desclée de Brouwer, Paris, 1949), pp. 17off.; Cornelius Van Til, *The New Modernism: An Appraisal of the Theology of Barth and Brunner* (James Clarke, 1946), pp. 137ff. It should be pointed out that in varying degrees these scholars contrast the transcendence of the personal divine Word of God with the human words of the biblical writers in Barth's teaching. *Cf.* also on this Klaas Runia, *op. cit.*, pp. 18–56, 116–136; James Brown, *Subject and Object in Modern Theology. The Croall Lectures given in the University of Edinburgh, 1953* (S.C.M. Press, 1955), on 'God Indissolubly Subject', pp. 140–167.

between God's transcendent freedom and everything finite and human.

Certainly, this was the view of Barth, the Dialectical Theologian.[2] But Barth's more recent writings seem to contain hints that this is still his view. There are the passages which distinguish the transcendent Word of God from the human words of the biblical writers.[3] The former is described as *pure act*; the latter are merely *witnesses* to revelation, whose word *becomes* the Word of God in the event of revelation. Above all, there is Barth's insistence that revelation is essentially God's revelation of Himself.

> What God utters is never in any way known and true in abstraction from God Himself. It is known and true for no other reason than that He Himself says it, that He in person is in and accompanies what is said by Him.[4]

This view has also the apparent added advantage of salvaging a biblical view of revelation without the embarrassment of having to defend 'the fatal doctrine of inspiration',[5] so unfashionable in many quarters.

But the Barth of today should not be saddled with the Barth of 1920.[6] The above points should not be ripped out of context. And in any case, what has been said so far is not the whole story. To put the question in perspective, certain further factors need to be taken into consideration.

(i) *Personal and propositional truth*. In the first place Barth himself does not subscribe to Temple's antithesis between personal and propositional:

> Thus God reveals Himself in propositions by means of language, and human language at that, to the effect that from time to time such and such a word, spoken by the

[2] See above, pp. 17–20.
[3] See above, pp. 21, 29–33.
[4] *C.D.*, I, 1, p. 155.
[5] *C.D.*, I, 1, p. 128; cf. *C.D.*, I, 2, pp. 503–526.
[6] Already in the Author's Preface to the English edition of *The Epistle to the Romans* (p. vi) Barth asks his readers not to bind the Professor at Bonn too closely to the Pastor at Safenwil. He wrote that in 1932. Since then his thought has not remained static. He would have even greater cause to write the same today.

prophets and apostles and proclaimed in the Church, becomes His Word. Thus the personality of the Word of
God is not to be played off against its verbal character and
spirituality.[7]

Barth is well aware of the fact that the sort of approach
typified by Temple's remarks creates more problems than it
solves. It reduces Scripture to being the purely human objec-
tification of subjective feeling-states.[8] In other words, the
prophetic: 'Thus saith the Lord', and the dominical: 'But
I say unto you' are terminologically inexact, if they are
taken at face value as expressions of the mind of God. God
does not and cannot speak at all. It would have been more
appropriate had the prophets said, 'My interpretation of
this event is . . .', or 'I have an overpowering impression
that . . .'

Temple summed up his view by saying: 'What is offered
to man's apprehension in any specific Revelation is not truth
concerning God but the living God Himself.'[9] His words
sound attractive. In fact, they are too glib. His approach
appears to assume that facts and language are a barrier to
personality. In point of fact, they are our principal means
of self-expression and communication. It is true that our
personalities cannot be compressed into propositions. It is
also true that unless we express ourselves in language, our
attempts to express ourselves become a dumb charade. To
deprive a person of language and the capacity to make himself articulate is to make that person sub-personal. There is
no *a priori* reason why the personal God should not be able
to express Himself in personal language.[1] And the biblical

---

[7] *C.D.*, I, 1, p. 156.

[8] This, in fact, appears to be the view of Peter Munz, *Problems of Religious Knowledge* (S.C.M. Press, 1959), p. 126.

[9] *Op. cit.*, p. 322.

[1] '*Personal*ness means being the subject not only in the logical sense, but also in the ethical sense, being a *free* subject, free even in respect of the periodical limitations which are given with its individuality as such, able to *dispose* of its own existence and nature, as much in so far as it is an express form, as in so far as it is a living development; but free also to *choose* new possibilities of existence and nature. If we represent to ourselves what that means, it will not occur to us to see in this personalising of the concept of the Word of God a case of anthropomorphism. The problem is not whether God is a person, the problem is whether we are' (*C.D.*, I, 1, p. 157).

writers attest this.[2] The implication of Temple's words is not to make God more personal, but to make Him less so.

In recognizing that God reveals Himself in language, Barth is not shutting his eyes to the fact that God reveals Himself in events and actions.[3] He would no more wish to deny this than he would want to deny that human personality is revealed in events and actions. The two are not mutually exclusive but complementary.

There is, however, a significant difference between human words and actions on the one hand and God's words and actions on the other. In the case of men, we can draw a distinction between a word as 'the mere self-utterance of a person' and an act as 'a relative alteration in the environment which proceeds from it'.[4] But with God His Word is also action. 'Where God speaks, it is meaningless to cast about for the corresponding act . . . The Word of God is itself the act of God.'[5]

(ii) *Faith*. Another factor to be considered when we try to appreciate Barth's understanding of revelation is his view of *faith*. Faith, after all, is the corollary of revelation, the positive human response which revelation seeks.

In *The Epistle to the Romans* Barth could describe faith as 'awe in the presence of the divine incognito'.[6] It corresponded to a Kierkegaardian conception of an utterly transcendent God who always remained *Wholly Other* and aloof,

[2] The above criticisms are not intended to preclude the possibility that the Word of God ever comes to man as the crystallizing of profound but hitherto inchoate convictions. The point at issue here is not the psychological processes lying behind the prophetic word but the finished product, as when the prophets said, 'Thus saith the Lord . . .' They were claiming that God was actually saying what their words were saying. The revelation was not some inarticulate experience or event at which their human words were groping. The mind and character of God were revealed precisely in and through these words.

[3] *Cf. C.D.*, I, 1, pp. 162–184.

[4] *C.D.*, I, 1, p. 164.

[5] *C.D.*, I, 1, pp. 162f. Among the biblical passages Barth discusses in this connection are Psalm 33:9; Isaiah 55:10f.; Jeremiah 23:29; Matthew 4:4; Romans 1:16; 1 Corinthians 1:18; Hebrews 4:12; James 1:18; 1 Peter 1:23ff.; 1 John 2:14; and the significance of the Word of God *coming* to the Old Testament prophets, as in Jeremiah 1 (*cf. C.D.*, I, 1, pp. 163–174).

[6] *Op. cit.*, p. 39.

a God who never identified Himself with anything in the
world. 'Now, Spirit is the denial of direct immediacy. If
Christ be very God, He must be unknown, for to be known
directly is the characteristic mark of an idol.'[7] The gospel,
Barth went on to say, 'does not expound or recommend
itself. It does not negotiate or plead, or threaten or make
promises.'[8] Admittedly, there is an element of trust and commitment in this conception of faith. But when we ask what
this really means, the answer seems to be that it is a matter
of launching out in confidence into the unknowable.[9]

But by the time Barth came to define faith in the *Church
Dogmatics* his emphasis had significantly shifted. The key
factor in this change is that faith has now a definite object.

> But it is the Word, it is Christ, to whom faith is *related*,
> because He *gives* Himself as object to it, who makes faith
> into faith, into real experience. Of course, because He
> *gives* Himself to it as object! For faith is not already faith
> because it has or is a relation – it might in fact be an
> objectless relation with an imagined object – but because
> the Word of God is given to it as the object of this con-
> nection, as the object of acknowledgment and therewith
> as the ground of real faith.[1]

In the first instance the object of faith is Christ. But as we
have just seen, people express themselves chiefly through
their words. Apart from language they remain largely un-
intelligible and even sub-personal. And apart from trust in
a person through his words, faith would remain blind self-

---

[7] *Ibid.*, p. 38, quoting Kierkegaard.   [8] *Ibid.*, pp. 38f.
[9] 'Faith is awe in the presence of the divine incognito; it is the love of God
that is aware of the qualitative distinction between God and man and God
and the world; it is the affirmation of the resurrection as the turning-point of
the world; and therefore of the divine "No" in Christ, of the shattering halt
in the presence of God . . . This discovery is, however, a free choice between
scandal and faith, a choice presented to him always and everywhere and at
every moment. Depth of feeling, strength of conviction, advance in perception and moral behaviour, are no more than things which accompany the
birth of faith. Being of this world, they are in themselves no more than un-
important signs of the occurrence of faith' (*op. cit.*, p. 39). In saying this much,
Barth has in fact said more than his premises strictly allow (see above, pp.
20ff.).
[1] *C.D.*, I, 1, p. 263.

committal. Barth, therefore, parts company with his former
existentialist views and returns to the orthodox conception
of the Reformers, which sees faith essentially as *none other
than trust in the promise of mercy.*

This particular definition is that of Melanchthon.[2] But it
could be matched by other similar ones drawn from the
writings and confessions of the other Reformers.[3] What is
important is that this concept contains the elements of cog-
nition (or *notitia* in the Latin used by the Reformers), assent
(*assensus*) and trust, commitment (*fiducia*). These are not
to be played off against each other, any more than the Word
incarnate should be played off against the Word written. In
true faith each element has its part to play.

This emphasis on *fiducia* is meant to mark off real faith
from a mere *opinio historica*, from a neutral recollective
knowledge and affirmation of Biblical or Church statements, such as is possible even apart from the reality of
faith. To exclude from faith the element of *notitia* or
assensus, i.e. the element of knowledge, to conceive of
faith as pure trust, which is intellectually without form or,
in view of its intellectual form, indifferent, as any kind of
trust in any kind of thing, to make the object of faith
problematic and to transfer the reality of faith to the
believing subject, was a possibility which we can say with
certainty . . . that even in the early period of the Reformation none of its responsible leaders took it seriously for
one single minute . . . But how should it be *fiducia* without at the same time and because it is *fiducia*, being
notitia and *assensus* too, *fiducia promissionis*, trust in the
mercy of God which meets us as the *misericordia promissa*,
i.e. in that objectivity of the Word, which has form and
the form of the Word at that, and therefore in the faith
that adopts it the form of knowledge also, the form of
conviction?[4]

---

[2] '*Est itaque fides non aliud, nisi fiducia misericordiae promissae*' (Melanchthon,
Loci, 1521, *De justificatione et fide*, IV; *cf. C.D.*, I, 1, p. 268).
[3] *Cf.* Calvin, 'Take away the Word and then no faith will remain' (*Institutes
of the Christian Religion*, III, ii, 6). For Barth's detailed discussion of faith in
the Reformers and other theologians see *C.D.*, I, 1, pp. 265–270.
[4] *C.D.*, I, 1, pp. 268f.

Having said this, it has also to be admitted that Barth's review of the biblical concept of faith is not as exhaustive as it might have been.[5] Nevertheless, it is instructive to compare Barth with William Temple, especially in view of the contrast we have already drawn with regard to their differing views of revelation.[6] When, in his *Readings in St. John's Gospel*, Temple came across passages in John which suggest faith involves response to propositional revelation his mind usually veered away from grasping the implications of the text, and he found other things to comment upon.[7]

But if we follow the Reformers and the New Testament, we shall not be embarrassed by the idea of revealed truth, or see any inherent contradiction between it and faith. In a very real sense the biblical idea of faith is a matter of living by the promises of God. For it is through the written Word that the incarnate Word becomes intelligible and indeed becomes capable of being the object of trust and commitment.

(iii) Analogy. The third factor to be considered in trying to appreciate and assess Barth's teaching on revelation is his doctrine of *analogy*. To see the relevance and force of Barth's teaching, it will be useful to sketch in something of the background of the debate between contemporary linguistic

---

[5] Barth takes *faith* in Romans 12:6; Galatians 1:23; 3:22f.; 1 Timothy 4:1, 6; Jude 3 to be 'the teaching of faith, the Gospel revealed to man, and so the path on which, starting from God, knowledge of God is made possible to him by His making Himself known' (*C.D.*, I, 1, p. 261). For a detailed account of faith in Scripture see the article on *faith* and its cognates by R. Bultmann and A. Weiser in *Theologisches Wörterbuch zum Neuen Testament*, founded by G. Kittel and edited by G. Friedrich, VI (Kohlhammer, Stuttgart, n.d.), pp. 174, 230; Eng. tr. *Faith* by D. M. Barton edited by P. R. Ackroyd (Black, 1961). The article instances the following as examples of the verb $\pi\iota\sigma\tau\epsilon\acute{\nu}\omega$ where the object is the written or spoken Word of God: Luke 1:20, 45; 24:25; John 2:22; 5:46f.; Acts 24:14; 26:27; 27:25. The noun $\pi\acute{\iota}\sigma\tau\iota\varsigma$ functions as a faith which is believed in Acts 6:7; Ephesians 4:5; 1 Timothy 1:19; 3:9; 4:1, 6; Jude 3, 20. In Romans 10:9; Galatians 3:23 faith is identified with acceptance of the kerygma.

[6] See above, pp. 41ff.

[7] (*First and Second Series*) (Macmillan, 1939–40), one-volume edition (1945, 1952). Cf., e.g., pp. 40f., 117–119, 392f.

philosophers and theologians.[8] Admittedly, Barth did not work out his teaching with this debate in mind. Nevertheless, Barth touches a number of points which British philosophers of religion have tended to overlook, and in the opinion of the present writer, Barth's teaching contains the elements of a solution to the problem posed by the philosophers.

In the 1920s and 1930s the Logical Positivists tried to cut the ground from underneath the theologians by claiming that the only truth was scientific truth which could be verified by controlled experiment. They went a step further than the old-fashioned atheist and agnostic who claimed that the arguments of religious people were false. The Logical Positivists held that these were in the first place meaningless nonsense, since concepts such as God and life after death had been generated by a misuse of language, which really applies only to the objects of sense-experience.

It was soon realized that the criteria of the Positivists backfired against themselves, for they had not been subjected to the empirical verification they demanded of others, and people found good meaning in many forms of utterances which the Positivists had ruled out of court. But ever since then philosophers and theologians have been engaged in a quest to ascertain what sort of meaning should be attached to religious language. Obviously, language about God is not literally true. When we speak about the Lamb of God, we do not mean a four-legged woolly animal. When Christians call God their Father they mean something rather different from what we mean by a human father. The latter is a man, usually not more than six feet tall, living in time and space, who has begotten children by natural procreation, *etc.* God is none of these things. The agnostic philosopher claims that when we press religious language to see what it

---

[8] On this see E. L. Mascall, *Words and Images: A Study in Theological Discourse* (Longmans, 1957); Basil Mitchell (ed.), *Faith and Logic: Oxford Essays in Philosophical Theology* (Allen and Unwin, 1957); Ian T. Ramsey, *Religious Language: An Empirical Placing of Theological Phrases* (S.C.M. Press, 1957); Frederick Copleston, *Contemporary Philosophy: Studies of Logical Positivism and Existentialism* (Burns and Oates, 1956); Frederick Ferré, *Language, Logic and God* (Eyre and Spottiswoode, 1962); Antony Flew and Alasdair MacIntyre (editors), *New Essays in Philosophical Theology* (S.C.M. Press, 1955).

really means, it dies a death of a thousand qualifications, so that in the end it is meaningless nonsense.

It would seem that three possible basic types of meaning are open to theological statements. On the one hand, they may be *univocal*, in which case the term always means the same in every context. On the other hand, they might be *equivocal*, in which case two or more terms have the same sound, but have entirely different meanings. Thus a mug is both a drinking utensil and the victim of a fraud. Obviously, neither of these two possibilities is a really live option for theological language. The former would reduce God to the level of a human being in the manner which we have just rejected.[9] The latter would make language about God utterly irrelevant. For though words about God might mean something on a human level, the reality to which they referred would be something quite different. It would be just as appropriate to recite *Baa, Baa, Black Sheep* as to utter the most solemn theological truths. But if we treat God as really *Wholly Other* to our language and thought-forms, one set of words is just as good or bad as another. Theology, preaching and witness are all equally a waste of time.

There remains the possibility that our language about God is in some sense *analogical*. In other words, when we call God our *Father*, He is neither wholly like nor wholly unlike human fathers, but there are genuine points of similarity.

Recognition of this truth is by no means new, but from time to time it has been forgotten or taken for granted. In the Middle Ages Thomas Aquinas recognized the essentially analogical nature of religious language.[1] In recent years it has been taken up again by Neo-Thomists on the one hand

---

[9] It is questionable whether any of our everyday language is strictly univocal except in the general, wide sense that common nouns have the same broad meaning. But even a word like *table* has a wide variety of meanings. Apart from different types of tables in domestic and other use, we speak of time-tables and tabling amendments. In the strictest sense perhaps only such forms of communication as mathematical symbols, chemical formulae and musical notation are univocal. Even the latter is not absolutely univocal for different musicians are able to put different interpretations on the same composition.

[1] *Summa Theologiae*, I, Q. 13; *Summa Contra Gentiles*, I, 34; *De Veritate*, 2, 11.

and Barthians on the other.[2] But in fact, analogy is implicit
in the parables of the kingdom, where the kingdom of God
is said to be like this or that. Throughout the Bible there is
the recognition that we do not normally in this life ever
have a direct vision of God as He is in Himself. Our knowledge of God is always veiled or refracted. God Himself does
not appear to His people in the exodus from Egypt, but
leads them in the pillar of cloud and the pillar of fire.[3] Even
Moses is not granted a direct vision of God, for no man can
see God's face and live.[4] *Seeing* God is something reserved
for the future for the pure in heart.[5] Knowledge in this life
is always imperfect.[6] It will, in fact, pass away.[7] 'For now we
see in a mirror dimly, but then face to face. Now I know
in part; then I shall understand fully, even as I have been
fully understood.'[8] Only love abides.[9] Truth is not only incomplete; it is given indirectly. Ultimate truth is always
refracted or veiled in human words and finite concepts. It
has to be so, in order that it may be unveiled and revealed.
This is not to say that it is not truth. There is a real correspondence between words and what they are about.[1] But it
is not a literal truth:

> Thus we can, indeed, say what the Word of God is; but
> we must say it indirectly. We must recall the forms in
> which it is real for us and from these three forms which
> it takes infer *how* it is. That 'how' is the reflected image,
> attainable by man, of the unattainable nature of God. It
> is with this reflected image that we are here to be
> occupied.[2]

This truth illuminates our way.[3] But it is not the absolutely
pure light of God as He is in Himself, but the light which

---

[2] For recent discussions see E. L. Mascall, *He Who Is: A Study in Traditional
Theism* (Longmans, 1943, 1962), pp. 95-115; *Words and Images: A Study in
Theological Discourse* (Longmans, 1957), pp. 101-108; *Existence and Analogy:
A Sequel to 'He Who Is'* (Longmans, 1949); F. Ferré, *op. cit.*, pp. 67-77; John
McIntyre, 'Analogy' in *S.J.T.*, Vol. XII, No. 1, March 1959, pp. 1-20.

[3] Exodus 13:21f., *etc.*   [4] Exodus 33:18-23.
[5] Matthew 5:8; *cf.* Hebrews 12:14; 1 John 3:2; Revelation 22:4.
[6] 1 Corinthians 13:9.   [7] 1 Corinthians 13:8, 10.
[8] 1 Corinthians 13:12.   [9] 1 Corinthians 13:8, 13.
[1] *Cf. C.D.*, I, 1, p. 279.   [2] *C.D.*, I, 1, pp. 149f.
[3] *Dogmatics in Outline*, p. 25.

He refracts through His Word. It is, in the true Christian sense of the term, a mystery.

> *Mysterium* signifies not simply the hiddenness of God, but rather His becoming manifest in a hidden, i.e. in a non-apparent way, which gives information not directly but indirectly. *Mysterium* is the veiling of God in which He meets us by actually unveiling Himself to us: because He will not and cannot unveil Himself to us in any other way than by veiling Himself.[4]

Barth's doctrine of analogy[5] differs from the Thomist doctrine of the analogy of being (*analogia entis*) in two major respects: its justification and its use. Both points are complementary.

The Catholic doctrine (at least as Barth sees it) is grounded upon rational reflection upon the nature of the universe, from which the existence of a supreme being was first deduced and then certain correspondence noted between finite being and the supreme being of which the latter was the ultimate cause. By contrast, Barth calls his doctrine an analogy of faith (*analogia fidei*).[6] For the only way of perceiving it is in faith. There are no means of knowing God apart from God revealing Himself in His Word through faith.[7] Analogy is given by revelation and perceived by faith. The only way of testing any given case of analogy is by comparing it with Scripture.

> Our alternative solution of the problem makes the claim to be sought and found not arbitrarily, but in orientation to the relationship between God and the creature, God and man, which we have normatively in the Holy Scriptures of the Old and New Testaments. In the Bible,

---

[4] *C.D.*, I, 1, p. 188.

[5] For Barth's teaching see *C.D.*, I, 1, pp. 11f., 274ff., 279f.; *C.D.*, II, 1, pp. 223–254.

[6] *C.D.*, I, 1, p. 279 and *passim*. Whether or not Paul has this in mind, as Barth thinks, in using the expression in Romans 12:6 is of infinitely less importance than the truth which he is trying to grasp by the term. Barth also speaks of an *analogia relationis* in connection with the image of God in man. But on this see below, pp. 112f.

[7] For Barth's rejection of natural theology, see below, pp. 77–98.

however, it is not a being common to God and man which
finally and properly establishes and upholds the fellowship between them, but God's grace. The presupposition
and criterion with which we entered on this problem of
analogy must therefore be considered in the light of this
fact . . . Scripture stands as judge between us and the
representatives of that other solution, and it can speak
for itself.[8]

As Barth's critics have not been slow to point out, an
analogy of being is implied in the analogy of faith.[9] There
must be some correspondence or there would be no analogy
at all. Indeed, as Barth recognizes, the doctrine ultimately
rests upon the doctrine of creation, in so far as God has
wrought a creation capable of reflecting His own being.[1]
But, as Barth also points out, the doctrine of creation is as

---

[8] *C.D.*, II, 1, p. 243.

[9] *Cf.* G. Söhngen, '*Analogia entis in analogia fidei*' in *Antwort*, pp. 266–271 and
W. Kreck, '*Analogia fidei oder analogia entis*', *ibid.*, pp. 272–286; Emil Brunner,
The Christian Doctrine of Creation and Redemption. Dogmatics, II, Eng. tr. by Olive
Wyon (Lutterworth, 1952), pp. 42–45. J. McIntyre thinks that the term
analogia gratiae would serve Barth better, for *analogia fidei* suggests 'something
created by our subjective act of faith; whereas it is because grace sets up the
analogy that faith takes place' (*op. cit.*, p. 15). Emil Brunner has also objected
to Barth's term on the grounds that Barth is using it in a private, special
sense, whereas in classical Protestant usage it denotes the method of expounding obscure passages of Scripture in the light of those whose meaning is
clear (*Revelation and Reason: The Christian Doctrine of Faith and Knowledge*, Eng.
tr. by Olive Wyon (S.C.M. Press, 1947), p.80). On Barth's doctrine see also
Hans Urs von Balthasar, *Karl Barth. Darstellung und Deutung seiner Theologie*
(Hegner-Bücherei, Olten, 1951), pp. 93–181; Karl Hammer, '*Analogia
relationis gegen analogia entis*' in *Parrhesia*, pp. 288–304; B. Mondin, *The
Principle of Analogy in Protestant and Catholic Theology* (Nijhoff, The Hague,
1963).

[1] 'For example, the words "father" and "son" do not first and properly have
their truth at the point of reference to the underlying views and concepts in
our thought and language, i.e. in their application to the two nearest male
members in the succession of physical generation of man or of animal creation
generally. They have it first and properly at a point to which, as our words,
they cannot refer at all, but to which, on the basis of the grace of the revelation of God, they may refer, and on the basis of the lawful claim of God
the Creator they even must refer, and therefore on the basis of this permission
and compulsion, they can actually refer – in their application to God, in the
doctrine of the Trinity. In a way which is incomprehensible and concealed
from us, but in the incontestable priority of the Creator over the creature,
God himself is *the* Father and *the* Son' (*C.D.*, II, 1, p. 229).

much a revealed doctrine as (say) the doctrines of the Trinity and the atonement.[2] And knowledge of analogy is a matter of grace and revelation.

> In His revelation God controls His property, elevating our words to their proper use, giving Himself to be their proper object, and therefore giving them truth. Analogy of truth between Him and us is present in His knowing, which comprehends ours, which does not comprehend His. But in our knowing, this analogy of truth comes into being in virtue of the decision of His grace, which is to this extent the grace of His revelation. It is not the case that we can anticipate or handle this divine control, elevating and giving; that even prior to God's decision, or without it, we can understand our truth as secondary to His and therefore His truth in the reflection of ours, our words as inexhaustible, as words that properly mean God.[3]

Conversely, Barth regards the doctrine of the *analogia entis* as 'the invention of Antichrist', and the chief reason for not becoming a Roman Catholic. For he sees this doctrine as the root of all Rome's doctrinal errors. By starting with man and what seems right to him, it has been used to make God in the image of man. The result is such hybrid errors as 'faith and works', 'nature and grace', 'reason and revelation', 'Scripture and tradition'.[4]

In introducing this section on Barth's teaching on analogy, I said that I believed that it contains the elements of a solution to the problem of the meaning of religious language. Both terms – elements and solution – are operative. Barth outlines the principle of analogy. He does not go on to discuss in detail how the mind grasps and perceives the truth of the biblical analogies and how they fit into the total

---

[2] See below, pp. 110; *cf. Dogmatics in Outline*, p. 50; *C.D.*, III, 1, pp. 3ff. *Cf.* Hebrews 11:3.

[3] *C.D.*, II, 1, p. 230.

[4] *C.D.*, I, 1, pp. x, 43f.; *cf. C.D.*, I, 2, p. 557; *C.D.*, II, 1, pp. 582f. It must be added that Roman Catholic theologians strongly reject the idea that Catholic teaching consciously uses the analogy of being in this way (*cf.* Hans Küng, *Justification: The Doctrine of Karl Barth and a Catholic Reflection* (Burns & Oates, 1966), p. 3).

structure of language.[5] But Barth does make the valid recognition that biblical images and analogies are not ends in themselves but are God-given means through which the mind perceives the truth which they represent.

It is all too possible for the mind to stop short at the literal aspect of the image. An obvious example of this is the doctrine of transubstantiation which has come about through taking Christ's words at the Last Supper too literally. Like the parables of the kingdom, biblical analogies need to be balanced against each other. Over-concentration on one at the expense of others may distort its truth. To be meaningful, they also need to be grasped in experience. Indeed, for Barth, revelation is not fully revelation until the Word of God reaches its goal in illuminating the heart and mind. When we say that Christ is the Bread of Life,[6] the Light of the World,[7] the Good Shepherd[8] and the True Vine,[9] we are not speaking the literal truth. Christ is none of these things physically. But the Christian believer knows something of what these analogies really mean, because they have been revealed to him in the gospel which, in turn, has brought new experience and meaning to his life.

Christian orthodoxy has always regarded such images as revealed truths of the divinely inspired Word of Scripture. In trying to complete this general picture of Barth's view of revelation, we shall therefore ask what meaning Barth attaches to the *inspiration* of Scripture.

(*iv*) *The inspiration of Scripture.* In view of what we have already seen of Barth's view of revelation, it is not surprising that Barth insists that the inspiration of Scripture should be viewed in the context of the act of divine self-disclosure. He rightly sees it as one factor among many in the whole process of revelation. But his actual exposition of the subject[1] is a curious blend of real insight and half-truth.

---

[5] Studies of the mechanics of the working of religious language are contained in Ian Ramsey, *op. cit.*; E. L. Mascall, *Words and Images*; Austin Farrer, *The Glass of Vision*, Bampton Lectures for 1948 (Dacre Press, 1948).

[8] John 6:35.   [7] John 8:12.

[6] John 10:14.   [9] John 15:1.

[1] *C.D.*, I, 2, pp. 514–526.

A prime example of this is his definition of inspiration. Taking 2 Timothy 3 : 16 and 2 Peter 1 : 20f. as his starting-point, Barth proceeds, despite the texts themselves, to transfer the idea of inspiration from the God-guided character of the biblical documents themselves to the whole dynamic process of revelation embracing both the writer and the reader in the revealing act of the Holy Spirit:

This self-disclosure in its totality is *theopneustia*, the inspiration of the word of the prophets and apostles.[2]

What Barth has done is not to give a definition of inspiration but to define revelation in general. What he says is true in itself, but it is not exactly the point at issue. Instead of giving a detailed examination of the two passages in question or of the immense amount of data in Scripture on its character as the written Word of God, such as B. B. Warfield gave in his numerous writings,[3] Barth proceeds to discuss the general perspective of revelation in the light of two passages from Paul. The first of these, 2 Corinthians 3 : 4–18, has to do with the reader who cannot understand Scripture apart from the illuminating work of the Holy Spirit. The second, 1 Corinthians 2 : 6–16, is concerned with the preacher or writer who cannot discern the deep truths about God again apart from the illuminating work of the Holy Spirit. But within these terms of reference Barth has much to say that is valid and vital.

On the former passage Barth writes:

The Old Testament Scripture as such is described by Paul (v. 6) as γράμμα i.e. as that which is simply written and indeed prescribed as holy and necessary for salvation. There is *per se* no disqualification of Scripture in this

[2] *C.D.*, I, 2, p. 516.
[3] The most important of these have been collected and edited by Samuel G. Craig and published under the title, *The Inspiration and Authority of the Bible* (Marshall, Morgan and Scott, 1951). For briefer discussions of the relevant material see J. I. Packer, *'Fundamentalism' and the Word of God. Some Evangelical Principles* (I.V.F., 1958), pp. 75–114; *God has spoken. Revelation and the Bible* (Hodder, 1965); J. W. Wenham, *Our Lord's View of the Old Testament* (Tyndale Press, 1953, I.V.F., 1964[2]).

designation. Nor is there when Paul goes on to say that the γράμμα kills but the Spirit gives life. This is said in favour of the Spirit but not against Scripture, or only against a Scripture received and read without the Spirit. From this standpoint we ought calmly to reflect on Matthew 5: 17f., where it says that not one jot or tittle can pass from the law until it is completely fulfilled, and that therefore even the least of its commandments must not be 'broken'.[4]

He then goes on to suggest reasons why Paul took this view of Scripture:

It makes no difference that as such and apart from the work of the Holy Spirit the written not only does not minister life, but ministers death; indeed, in its own way it proves that it is and remains that which is prescribed by divine authority. Paul must have known the theories of Talmudic and Alexandrian Jewry concerning the divine-human origin of the Torah, i.e. all the Old Testament Canon. If, as we can certainly assume, he for his part affirmed a special inspiration of Scripture by God, it was obviously only in connexion with his view of the present attestation of the same God by the work of the Holy Spirit.[5]

There are two points here. On the one hand, inspiration is not something which comes and goes (as might be suggested by Barth's idea of Scripture *becoming* the Word of God[6]); it is something intrinsic to the documents. On the other hand, there is Paul's reason for affirming his belief in the inspired character of the Old Testament Scriptures. It lies in their self-authenticating character in view of the fact that God once spoke through them and continues to do so.[7]

Barth's comments on the other key passage, 1 Corinthians 2 : 6–16, reinforce this view.

As the human spirit knows human things, so it is the divine Spirit – He alone, but He perfectly and without doubt – who knows divine things. This Spirit he, Paul,

[4] *C.D.*, I, 2, p. 514.   [5] *C.D.*, I, 2, p. 515.
[6] See above, p. 32.   [7] See above, pp. 35ff., 39.

has received, that he may know as such the divine benefits of the divine wisdom (τὰ ὑπὸ τοῦ θεοῦ χαρισθέντα ἡμῖν, vv. 10–12). But as he sees it, this does not exhaust the work of the Holy Ghost. In exact correspondence with this knowledge of the benefits indicated to us by God's wisdom he now believes he can and must express them: οὐκ ἐν διδακτοῖς ἀνθρωπίνης σοφίας λόγοις, ἀλλ᾽ ἐν διδακτοῖς πνεύματος; not in the words which man's wisdom teacheth but which the Spirit teacheth: πνευματικοῖς πνευματικὰ συγκρίνοντες: measuring and embracing in spiritual words that spiritual reality (v. 13). In face of this self-utterance we cannot assume that Paul did not take account of an inspiration, even a real and verbal inspiration, of the Old Testament hagiographa. We have therefore no reason to think that the θεόπνευστος of 2 Timothy 3:16 is non-Pauline. At all events Paul distinctly describes himself, not merely as a witness of the divine benefits, so that his statements about them have the value of an historical record, but more than that, as one who by the Spirit is enabled and led to know these benefits, and even more, as one who by the same Spirit is authorised and taught to speak about them.[8]

On this basis Barth goes so far as to associate himself with the early church theologians, Clement of Alexandria and Gregory of Nazianzus, in extending inspiration to the phraseology and grammar of the biblical writers:

If I am right, the first express statement along these lines is to be found in the *Protrepticus* of Clement of Alexandria (IX, 82, 1): that the fact according to Matthew 5:18 that not even the slightest jot or tittle of Scripture can be destroyed is based on the truth that it has all been spoken by the mouth of the Lord, the Holy Spirit. And a hundred years later Gregory of Nazianzus (*Orat.* 2, 105) writes that every slightest line and stroke of Scripture is due to the minute care of the Spirit and that even the slenderest nuance of the writers is not in vain or displayed to us in vain. Here, too, in the light of Matthew 5:17f. we must be on our guard against trying to say anything different. If in their concrete existence and therefore in their concrete speaking and writing the witnesses of revelation belong to revelation, if they spoke by the Spirit what they knew by the Spirit, and if we really have to hear them and there-

[8] *C.D.*, I, 2, pp. 515f.

fore their words – then self-evidently we have to hear all
their words with the same measure of respect. It would be
arbitrary to relate their inspiration only to such parts of
their witness as perhaps appear important to us, or not to
their words as such but only to the views and thoughts
which evoke them.[9]

Having made this point, Barth then returns to his central
theme that revelation is encounter with the living God, and
therefore, that inspiration must not be taken out of the
context of the whole dynamic process of revelation. Otherwise, the Bible becomes a ' "paper Pope", and unlike the
living Pope in Rome . . . wholly given up into the hands of
its interpreters'.[1]

In the light of all this, it would seem that Barth is trying
to restate the position of Protestant orthodoxy in a way that
is dynamic, biblical and Christ-centred. Two important
differences emerge, however, when Barth's teaching is compared with that of the ancient upholders of verbal inspiration.[2] The one concerns Barth's view of *time*. We shall

[9] *C.D.*, I, 2, pp. 517f. (The English translation omits a sentence from the
German original citing Origen's comments on Psalm 1:4, but it retains
Barth's main thought.)

[1] *C.D.*, I, 2, p. 525.

[2] For the teaching of the Reformers see, *e.g.*, John Calvin, *Institutes of the
Christian Religion* (1559), in particular, Books I, vi-x, IV, viii-ix; H. Heppe,
Reformed Dogmatics, Set Out and Illustrated from the Sources, ed. E. Bizer, Eng. tr.
by G. T. Thomson (Allen and Unwin, 1950), pp. 12–46; 'A Fruitful Ex-
hortation to the Reading and Knowledge of Holy Scripture' in *The Homilies*,
Book I (1547); 'An Information for them that take Offence at certain Places
of the Holy Scripture' in *The Homilies*, Book II (1571). For further discussion
see especially *C.D.*, I, 2, pp. 518–526; J. K. S. Reid, *The Authority of Scripture.
A Study of the Reformation and Post-Reformation Understanding of the Bible*
(Methuen, 1957); T. H. L. Parker, *The Doctrine of the Knowledge of God: A
Study in the Theology of John Calvin* (Oliver and Boyd, 1952); E. A. Dowey, Jr.,
The Knowledge of God in Calvin's Theology (Columbia University Press, New York,
1952); B. B. Warfield, *Calvin and Augustine* (ed. Samuel G. Craig) (Presby-
terian and Reformed Publishing Co., Philadelphia, 1956), pp. 29–130,
387–477; C. Sydney Carter, *The Reformers and Holy Scripture: A Historical
Investigation* (Thynne and Jarvis, 1928); Philip Edgcumbe Hughes, *Theology of
the English Reformers* (Hodder, 1965); Robert Preus, *The Inspiration of Scripture:
A Study of the Theology of the Seventeenth Century Lutheran Dogmaticians* (Oliver
and Boyd, 1955, 1957[2]); F. Pieper, *Christian Dogmatics* (Concordia, St.
Louis, 1951), I, pp. 193–367. For a general survey of patristic views see
J. N. D. Kelly, *Early Christian Doctrines* (Black, 1958), pp. 29–79.

attempt to sketch his position in point (*v*) at the end of this section. The other concerns the question of the infallibility of Scripture.

For the Reformers and the early church the doctrine of verbal inspiration implied the collateral doctrine of in-errancy. Barth acknowledges the logical sequence of this thought, but denies its validity:

> To the bold postulate, that if their word is to be the Word of God they must be inerrant in every word, we oppose the even bolder assertion, that according to the scriptural witness about man, which applies to them too, they can be at fault in any word, and have been at fault in every word, and yet according to the same scriptural witness, being justified and sanctified by grace alone, they have still spoken the Word of God in their fallible and erring human word.[3]

> The prophets and apostles as such, even in their office, even in their function as witnesses, even in the act of writing down their witness, were real, historical men as we are, and therefore sinful in their action, and capable and actually guilty of error in their spoken and written word. If the miracle happened to them that they were called to be witnesses of the resurrection and that they received the Holy Spirit, it was to them it happened, leaving them the full use of their human freedom and not removing the barriers which are therefore posited for them as for all of us.[4]

In other words, to err is human; the biblical writings are human documents; therefore they contain error.

Before proceeding to look at what practical consequences Barth draws, or (to be more exact) fails to draw from this, two observations may be made. The first is that the idea that the coming to us of the revealing Word in fallible human words appears to be a parallel to Barth's contention that, in order to be a true incarnation, Christ must assume *fallen* human nature.[5] Whether Barth gains anything by

---

[3] *C.D.*, I, 2, pp. 529f.   [4] *C.D.*, I, 2, pp. 528f.
[5] *C.D.*, I, 2, pp. 147–155.

making this latter paradoxical point is somewhat dubious, as
Barth goes on to insist that Christ was also sinless.[6] The
same might be asked of his view that to be truly human the
biblical documents must be fallible, especially in the light
of our second observation.

This is that far from being something novel and esoteric
the idea of infallibility is a factor of common speech and indeed is a presupposition of language. Infallibility means freedom from error: that what is said corresponds with fact. In
point of fact, *all* our assertions make a similar implicit claim.
Whether we say, 'I had cornflakes for breakfast', or whether
we couch our thought in some poetic figure such as 'I wan-
dered lonely as a cloud', we are asserting that there is a
true correspondence between our words and some aspect of
reality. Whether or not the claim is true depends not upon
the inherent structure of language or human nature in
general, but upon whether the words were used accurately.
Errors occur when, wittingly or unwittingly, we misuse
language. But in point of fact, much more of our everyday
speech could be described as *infallible* than we commonly
suppose, even though it might also be trivial! What distinguishes the doctrine of infallibility of Scripture from ordinary speech is the claim that the writers were so guided by
the Holy Spirit that what they wrote always corresponded
with the reality that the writers intended to describe, and
that in writing they were kept from falling into error.

The point of this digression is to draw attention to the
fact that this question cannot be settled by an *a priori*
appeal like Barth's to human nature's general weaknesses,
but only by examination of the documents themselves in
the light of their claims and what is known for certain about
the matters they purport to describe.[7]

It is interesting, therefore, that when it comes down to
actually handling Scripture, Barth prefers to speak of a
capacity for errors rather than of actual errors.[8] He goes on

---

[6] *C.D.*, I, 2, pp. 155ff. On this see D. M. Baillie, *God Was in Christ: An Essay on
Incarnation and Atonement* (Faber, 1948, 1954⁵), pp. 16ff.

[7] On this question see further J. I. Packer, *'Fundamentalism' and the Word of
God*, pp. 94–101.

[8] *C.D.*, I, 2, p. 508.

to say that the Bible's 'capacity for error, also extends to its religious or theological content'.[9] But in practice he finds it impossible to say what is erroneous and what is not:

There are obvious overlappings and contradictions – e.g. between the Law and the prophets, between John and the Synoptists, between Paul and James. But nowhere are we given a single rule by which to make a common order, perhaps an order of precedence, but at any rate a synthesis, of what is in itself such a varied whole. Nowhere do we find a rule which enables us to grasp it in such a way that we can make organic parts of the distinctions and evade the contradictions as such. We are led now one way, now another – each of the biblical authors obviously speaking only *quod potuit homo* – and in both ways, and whoever is the author, we are always confronted with the question of faith. Again, we must be careful not to be betrayed into taking sides, into playing off the one biblical man against the other, into pronouncing that this one or that has 'erred'. From what standpoint can we make any such pronouncement?[1]

Having made his point, Barth is as good as his word. This is not to say that his biblical exegesis is always immaculate. But in practice he does not start out with the assumption that this or that writer is mistaken or conditioned by his background so that his witness is *a priori* irrelevant. Nor does Barth play off one writer against another. He seeks to follow the rule we have seen him already lay down, that we should listen to all the writings of all the writers 'with the same measure of respect' and treat them all as equally inspired.[2]

But this only makes the problem of the authority of Scripture more acute. It means that we should treat Scripture as both true and false at the same time. It is true in so far as

<hr />

[9] *C.D.*, I, 2, p. 509.   [1] *Ibid.*

[2] *C.D.*, I, 2, p. 517 (*cf.* above, p. 58). When Barth visited the United States in 1962 the question of errors in Scripture came into prominence. Replying to criticisms of his father, Professor Markus Barth of the University of Chicago wrote in *Christianity Today*: 'Do you realize that my father has never said, either in his Dogmatics or in the Panel Discussions in Chicago, that the Bible *does* err? *Christianity Today* always gave the impression as if in so many words he had said precisely this.' In reply a correspondent drew attention to some of the passages noted above (*cf.* Gordon H. Clark, *op. cit.*, p. 188, n. 1.)

God speaks through any and every word. It is false in so far
as those same words may be factually mistaken. Barth's view
of Scripture is sometimes presented as a way out of the
deadlock between the traditional, orthodox view and the
liberal, critical approach. But the double-think prescribed
by the remedy is more intolerable than the ailment. This
crack at the very foundation of Barthian dogmatics may ultimately prove to be the greatest obstacle to a more general
acceptance of Barth's doctrine of revelation. However, there
is another possibility, which is that Barth himself does not
take the question of error very seriously. It may be little
more than a token offering of respect to the critical spirit of
the age. Certainly, having devoted a few pages of the *Dogmatics* to it, it is not a question which appears to weigh
heavily on Barth's mind. In practice he seems to revert to
the traditional Reformed approach to Scripture. But Barth's
position is not really satisfying. At best it is an uncomfort-
able stop-gap solution. It is impossible to maintain high
doctrines of revelation and inspiration without at the same
time being willing to defend in detail the veracity and
historicity of the biblical writings. And this is something
which Barth neglects to do.[3]

(v) *Time.* In comparing Barth's views on inspiration with
the teaching of Protestant orthodoxy, it was suggested above[4]
that Barth differs from the latter over the question of in-
errancy and also in his emphasis on time. It is the belief of
the present writer that the place occupied in Reformed
orthodoxy by the doctrine of verbal inspiration is filled in
Barth by his doctrine of time. Admittedly, Barth has, as we
have just seen, a doctrine of verbal inspiration which in
practice is never very far from the surface of his thinking.
But his doctrine of time bulks much larger in his discussions.[5] Moreover, the need which the two doctrines seek to
meet in their respective theologies is largely the same. This

[3] For fuller discussion of this whole subject see Gordon H. Clark, *op. cit.*, pp.
189–225; Klaas Runia, *op. cit.*, pp. 57–115.
[4] See above, p. 58.
[5] For Barth's exposition of the subject see especially *C.D.*, I, 2, pp. 45–121;
C.D., III, 2, pp. 437–640; *C.D.*, IV, 1, pp. 286ff., 318ff., 725–739.

is the need to show how God's Word written in the past still speaks to us in our contemporary situation. The orthodox doctrine of inspiration meets it by showing that the Bible is God's Word to man, indeed His last word on the things that really matter. Barth's doctrine of time tries to explain how the free, eternal, living God encounters men in that ever-changing process which we call time. Again it must be stressed that for Barth the two doctrines are not mutually exclusive. But the question of time is something which previous generations of Christian thinkers have tended to overlook, and which Barth considers to be of the greatest importance. What follows here is little more than an extended footnote, merely attempting to set out Barth's views. The subject itself deserves much fuller consideration.[6]

Barth's approach appears to be determined by two factors, both of which date from his early Dialectical Theology. One is his view that revelation is a dynamic, personal process. The other is that the truth of revelation is not something immanent which man has within his grasp and which for that very reason is ultimately transitory and sinful. Rather it is something new and eternal which breaks into our lost situation.[7]

Barth argues that if we define time in terms of man and finite phenomena, the past (and with it God's actions and revelation in the past) just cease to be as soon as the present becomes past. As soon as we try to look at time it is either *not yet* or *no longer*.[8] For Barth, revelation creates a real

---

[6] Barth's concept of time was the subject of Dr. Klaas Runia's doctoral dissertation at the Free University of Amsterdam, *De Theologische Tijd bij Karl Barth*, 1955. Cornelius Van Til attempts to criticize Barth on philosophical grounds in *Christianity and Barthianism* (Presbyterian and Reformed, Philadelphia, 1962), pp. 90–113. *Christ and Time. The Primitive Christian Conception of Time and History* by Oscar Cullmann, Eng. tr. by Floyd V. Filson (S.C.M. Press, 1951, 1957) is to some extent a reply to Barth. For other modern discussions of time see John Marsh, *The Fulness of Time* (Nisbet, 1952); James Barr, *Biblical Words for Time* (S.C.M. Press, 1962); and *The Semantics of Biblical Language* (O.U.P., 1961, 1962), pp. 46–88; T. Boman, *Hebrew Thought Compared with Greek*, Eng. tr. by J. L. Moreau (S.C.M. Press, 1960); and F. W. Camfield, 'Man in his Time' in *S.J.T.*, Vol. III, No. 2, 1950, pp. 127–148.

[7] *Cf. C.D.*, I, 1, p. 168; *C.D.*, I, 2, pp. 67ff.

[8] *C.D.*, I, 2, p. 52. *Cf.* Barth's discussion of philosophical concepts of time in *C.D.*, I, 1, pp. 166f.; *C.D.*, I, 2, pp. 45ff.

time which, while breaking into our 'lost time', nevertheless exists over and above it.

The time God has for us is constituted by His becoming present to us in Jesus Christ, i.e. *Deus praesens*. If we say Jesus Christ, we also assert a human and therefore temporal presence. Every moment of the event of Jesus Christ is also a temporal moment, i.e. a present with a past behind it and a future in front of it, like the temporal moments in the sequence of which we exist ourselves. 'The Word became flesh' also means 'the Word became time' . . . So it is not a sort of ideal, yet in itself timeless content of all or some times. It does not remain transcendent over time, it does not merely meet it at a point, but it enters time; nay, it assumes time; nay, it creates time for itself.[9]

From here Barth proceeds to expound the Old Testament as the 'pre-time' of 'fulfilled time' or the 'time of expectation', and the New Testament as the 'time of recollection'.[1] Christ is present in both.[2] But the focal point of time, 'fulfilled time', the time of 'the pure presence of God',[3] is the period of Christ's resurrection appearances when Christ encountered His disciples in a unique way.

But the Easter story (with, if you like, the story of the transfiguration and the story of the conversion of Saul as

[9] *C.D.*, I, 2, p. 50.   [1] *C.D.*, I, 2, pp. 70–101 and 101–121.
[2] Barth holds that Christ, the revealing Word, comes through the witness of the Old Testament no less than that of the New. 'His promise in the Old Testament already signifies His real presence in the pre-time is shown by 1 Corinthians 10:1–4, which speaks about baptism and the Father's gift of spiritual meat and drink in the desert, and which says expressly of the rock from which they drank, ἡ πέτρα δὲ ἦν ὁ Χριστός (*C.D.*, I, 2, p. 74; *cf. C.D.*, I, 2, pp. 72ff. for Barth's exegesis of Matthew 5:17f.; Luke 1:54, 72; 10:24; 24:13–32; John 1:41, 45; 4:22; 5:39, 45ff.; 8:56; 12:37–41 (*cf.* Isaiah 6:9f.; 53:1); Acts 3:20f.; 8:16f. (*cf.* Isaiah 53); 10:43; 17:11; 26:22; Romans 1:2; 3:21, 31; 15:8; 2 Corinthians 3:14f.; Galatians 3:24; 1 Peter 1: 10ff. on the basis of which Barth interprets the Old Testament as a revelation of Christ. For a recent important study which follows much the same line as Barth (only without mentioning him) see A. T. Hanson, *Jesus Christ in the Old Testament* (S.P.C.K., 1965).
[3] *C.D.*, I, 2, p. 115.

prologue and epilogue respectively) actually speaks of a present without any future, of an eternal presence of God in time. So it does not speak eschatologically. The Easter story, Christ truly, corporeally risen, and as such appearing to His disciples, talking with them, acting in their midst – this is, of course, the recollection upon which all the New Testament recollections hang, to which they are all related, for the sake of which there is a New Testament recollection at all.[4]

Sometimes the suggestion is made that Barth takes the resurrection of Christ out of history.[5] In Barth's defence it may be admitted that he does not attempt a detailed historical investigation of the event in the manner of, say, James Orr's *The Resurrection of Jesus*,[6] and without which no answer to sceptical criticism is really complete. On the other hand, whatever we think Barth ought to say in the light of what we think to be his preconceived philosophy, he does here affirm Christ's physical resurrection in time. He goes on to say that it is 'quite indispensable' to the New Testament message and 'impossible to think away'.[7] Moreover, he treats the encounters with the risen Christ as a foretaste, a trailer or paradigm of what it will be like in the end time at the second coming of Christ.[8]

Oscar Cullmann's verdict on Barth's view of time describes it as 'the last but quite momentous remnant of the influence of philosophy upon his exposition of the Bible'.[9] In reply, Barth accuses Cullmann of overlooking the importance of the resurrection which, significantly, comes in only at the end of his book, and of construing time as an ascending line of aeons, intersected by the coming of Christ.[1] Rather, Barth insists that the resurrection of Christ which transcends the limitations of time and space is the 'vantage point' from

[4] *C.D.*, I, 2, p. 114; *cf. C.D.*, III, 2, p. 443.
[5] *Cf.* Cornelius Van Til, *op. cit.*, p. 109.
[6] Hodder, 1908.
[7] *C.D.*, I, 2, p. 114; *cf.* Barth's exegesis of Mark 16:8f.; Luke 24:48; Acts 1:8, 22ff.; 4:33; 1 Corinthians 15:14f. (*ibid.*, pp. 114f.).
[8] *C.D.*, IV, 1, pp. 333f.
[9] *Op. cit.*, p. 13.
[1] *C.D.*, III, 2, p. 443; *cf.* Cullmann, *op. cit.*, pp. 231ff.

which to judge time.[2] It is, moreover, the vantage point from which are to be judged all theologies and philosophies which seek to explain it away. Those which attempt to do this just fail to do justice to the New Testament.[3] The Christian faith is more than the inspiring mental recollection of something in the past which, when once over, entirely ceased to be. The Christian faith is faith in Him whose resurrection shows Him to be the Lord of time,[4] and whose 'resurrection is the anticipation of His *parousia* and His *parousia* is the completion and fulfilment of the resurrection'.[5]

d. Summary

A fuller appraisal of Barth's teaching on the Word of God will be attempted in the final chapter. But it may be worth while to pause briefly at this point and draw together the threads of the discussion so far. Barth's teaching on the Bible in the *Church Dogmatics* is a direct descendant of Dialectical Theology. And it bears the marks of its parentage. But in the last analysis it is an attempt to restate the position of the Reformers and of the Bible itself. The central themes that we noted in Barth's commentary on *The Epistle to the Romans* again recur: the freedom of God, the grace of God and the Christ-centredness of all revelation. It is the way that Barth works out these themes that constitutes his strength and weakness.

On the one hand, Barth insists that the Word of God is not simply an object; it is God Himself speaking. Therefore, although the historian can investigate the factual details of

---

[2] *Ibid.*

[3] On this basis Barth proceeds to criticize Bultmann's demythologizing of Easter (*C.D.*, III, 2, pp. 443–447). For a fuller critique see 'Rudolf Bultmann – An Attempt to Understand Him' in *Kerygma and Myth. A Theological Debate*, II, edited by Hans-Werner Bartsch, Eng. tr. by R. H. Fuller (S.P.C.K., 1962), pp. 83–132. See *C.D.*, I, 1, pp. 167f. for Barth's critique of earlier liberals who failed to appreciate Christ's 'contingent contemporaneousness'.

[4] *C.D.*, III, 2, p. 443; *cf.* 1 Timothy 1:17.

[5] *C.D.*, III, 2, p. 490 and the discussion on the following pages of such passages as 2 Peter 1:16–21 (p. 494); 1 Peter 1:3–12 (pp. 495ff.); Mark 9:1f. (p. 499); Matthew 10:23 (pp. 499f.); Mark 13:30 (pp. 500f.); Matthew 26:29 (p. 502); Matthew 25 (pp. 505ff.).

the Bible, he cannot in the last analysis use his techniques to judge the Word of God. The Word of God can only be appreciated in faith and obedience. For we miss the whole point of the Bible if we do not see it as the revelation of Christ. The words of the biblical writers are the words of specially commissioned witnesses to Christ who is the revelation of the Father. As we receive their divinely guided witness, we encounter Him who breaks into our situation in a new dimension. In all this it is God Himself who takes the initiative. He is the subject of revelation from first to last. Only in virtue of God being the subject can there be any objective revelation.

On the other hand, it is these insights which seem to prevent Barth from doing full justice to the claims of Scripture to be the written Word of God. Barth's willingness to draw a distinction between the Word of God itself and the fallible words of the Bible leads to the dilemma in which any given passage of the Bible is true in so far as it is the Word of God and false in so far as it is the erring word of man.

Barth's way out of this dilemma is to ignore it. In practice, if not quite in theory, he seems to return to the older orthodox method of treating the Bible as the divinely inspired Word of God. But this approach can only be defensible if at the same time one is able to defend the veracity and historicity of Scripture in the way that older orthodox theologians did and Evangelicals seek to do today.

Having said this, we have by no means exhausted what Barth has to say about the Word of God and the knowledge of God. We have yet to consider Barth's teaching on the Word of God and the doctrine of the Trinity.

III THE WORD OF GOD AND THE DOCTRINE OF THE TRINITY

a. The place of the doctrine of the Trinity in Barth's thinking

Handbooks on Christian doctrine usually begin with an account of their principles of authority and method. The main substance of their teaching on the nature of God, man, sin and salvation is normally prefaced by a discussion of the nature and source of theological knowledge. This is true of Charles Hodge and T. C. Hammond no less than of Calvin

and Aquinas.[6] The doctrine of the Trinity is put well down
in the batting order, so to speak, as part of the substance
proper of dogmatics.

Karl Barth stands this procedure on its head. For him the
principle of authority and method is nothing less than the
divine Trinity. If we want to understand the nature of
Christian truth, we must turn to the revelation of the Word
of God. And if we turn to the Word of God, we are at once
confronted with the Triune God:

> But if we mean by the word 'revelation' 'the Word became
> flesh and dwelt among us', then we are asserting something
> that is to be grounded only within the Trinity; namely, by
> the Will of the Father, by the mission of the Son and of
> the Holy Spirit, by the eternal decree of the Triune God,
> i.e. not otherwise than as the knowledge of God from God,
> as knowledge of the Light in the Light.[7]

The *Prolegomena* to Barth's *Church Dogmatics*, which takes
up both parts of the first volume of the work, is therefore a
massive study of the doctrine of the Trinity as it emerges
in relation to revelation. All that we have seen so far of the
place and function of Scripture is, Barth insists, to be seen
in the context of the Triune God's revelation of Himself.
Barth's formulation of the doctrine occupies the central
place in his *Prolegomena*.[8]

[6] *Cf.* T. C. Hammond, '*In Understanding Be Men*': *An Introductory Handbook on
Christian Doctrine* (I.V.F., 1936, 1954[5]); Charles Hodge, *Systematic Theology*,
I–III, 1871; John Calvin, *Institutes of the Christian Religion* (1559), I; Thomas
Aquinas, *Summa Theologiae*, I, Q. 1.

[7] *C.D.*, I, 1, p. 134.

[8] *C.D.*, I, 1, pp. 339–560; *C.D.*, I, 2, pp. 1–454. For an important study of
Barth's teaching see Claude Welch, *The Trinity in Contemporary Theology*
(S.C.M. Press, 1953), pp. 161–213. It is touched upon much more briefly in
R. S. Franks, *The Doctrine of the Trinity* (Duckworth, 1953), pp. 177–184. Barth
is well aware of the novelty of putting the doctrine of the Trinity at the head
of his dogmatics. So far as he is aware, precedent for this is confined to the
Sentences of Peter Lombard and the *Breviloquium* of Bonaventura in the Middle
Ages. But, he explains: 'Our reason for deviating from this custom is this. It
is difficult to see how in regard of Holy Scripture we can tell what is significant
for the holiness of this very Scripture, unless previously it has been made clear
– naturally from Holy Scripture itself – who that God is whose revelation
makes Scripture Holy. And again, it is difficult to see how what is significant
for this God should be made clear, if, as has been done repeatedly in old and

b. Revelation as 'the root of the doctrine of the Trinity'[9]

The starting-point of Barth's thinking is the thought that
revelation is something which only God can do. Only God
can reveal God. This is what Barth means when he says that
in revelation, 'God reveals Himself as Lord'.[1] 'Godhead in
the Bible', he explains, 'means freedom, ontic and noetic
independence.'[2] In other words, man by himself can do nothing to obtain or pass on to others the knowledge of God.
God remains sovereign in His gracious act of revealing
Himself. But when we analyse what Scripture says about
this act of sovereign grace, we are confronted not with a
single, absolute, ultimate principle, but a threefold Lordship: that of the Father, that of the Son and that of the
Holy Spirit.

In the first instance, the Bible and indeed Jesus are concerned with revealing the Lordship of the Father. As Barth
says, 'True and real *divinity*, as expressed in the predicate
Kyrios, the NT already ascribes in the first instance to a
completely *Other* than Jesus.'[3] His biblical exegesis on the
following pages amply proves the point.[4]

But the New Testament writings also bear witness to Jesus
Christ as Lord. Barth is well aware of the fact that the title
was bestowed upon the divine rulers of Hellenistic Egypt,
the cult gods of Syria and even Roman emperors, so that in
the ancient world it could mean virtually anything or nothing. But, he rightly points out, this could hardly be the case
in the primitive church where the Old Testament name for

---

new Catholic and Protestant dogmatics, we reserve the question to which the
doctrine of the Trinity is the answer (namely, *Who God* is) and deal first with
His *existence* and His *nature*, as if this That and What could be determined
otherwise than on the presupposition of the *Who*' (*C.D.*, I, 1, p. 345).

[9] The phrase is taken from one of Barth's section headings (*C.D.*, I, 1, pp.
349–383).

[1] *C.D.*, I, 1, p. 351.   [2] *C.D.*, I, 1, p. 352.   [3] *C.D.*, I, 1, p. 442.

[4] See Barth's comments on Mark 10:18; 14:36; 15:34; Matthew 12:18;
Acts 3:13, 26; 4:27, 30; John 14:6, 28; 17:3; 1 Corinthians 3:23; 8:6; 11:3;
15:24; 2 Corinthians 4:4; Ephesians 2:18; Philippians 2:11; Colossians 1:15;
Hebrews 1:3; 3:2; 5:7f.; 9:14 in *C.D.*, I, 1, pp. 442f.; and his whole discussion of God the Father in *C.D.*, I, 1, pp. 441–56.

God, Yahweh-Adonai, was deliberately applied to Jesus.[5] The very name of Jesus also points in this direction. For in this name all manner of acts are performed in the New Testament which one would expect to be performed in the name of God. In the context of all that is done in this name it 'bears pretty much the same, comprehensive, pervasive meaning which the name Yahweh has in the O.T.: the name of Yahweh is just *Yahweh manifest to men*'.[6] In similar vein is the meaning of the title 'Son of God' which 'was a widespread designation in the ancient East simply for the king. But the context of New Testament Christology makes this title also eloquent in quite a definite way.'[7]

All these titles are understood in the New Testament in the context of what Jesus Christ both says and does. He is the one who brings about reconciliation between God and

---

[5] *C.D.*, I, 1, p. 458. Barth does not go into details on this, but the juxtaposition of the questions of the great commandment and David's son (Matthew 22:34–45) is a significant example. Jesus says that the great commandment is to love *the Lord your God* to the utmost. But immediately he points to another who is also Lord, according to Psalm 110. 'How is it then that David, inspired by the Spirit, calls him Lord, saying, "The Lord said to my Lord . . ."?'

[6] 'We are pointed in the same direction by the practical *meaning* of the name of Jesus, as the name in which they prophesied, taught, preached, prayed, baptised, in which sins were forgiven, devils driven out, and other miracles performed, in which His followers must assemble, in which they must admit each other, in which they must believe, upon which they must call, by which they must remain stedfast, for the sake of which they must indeed be even hated and scorned, and lose every earthly possession, in fact perhaps even die; in which, once more, they are also "washed, sanctified, justified" (1 Corinthians 6:11), which, so to speak, is the place, the region in which their entire language and action should take place' (Colossians 3:17) (*ibid.*). Barth does not supply further biblical references to these points, but they can be readily found. An obvious example is the episode in Mark 2:2–12 where Jesus heals a paralytic by saying 'Your sins are forgiven'. This provokes the comment which Jesus accepts: 'Why does this man speak thus? It is blasphemy! Who can forgive sins but God alone?'

[7] See Barth's exegesis of Matthew 11:27f.; 16:16; 26:63f.; John 1:1–18; 5:17f., 26; 8:58; 10:30; 14:9; 17:24; Acts 10:36; 1 Corinthians 8:6; 2 Corinthians 5:19f.; Philippians 2:6; Colossians 1:13, 16; 2:9; Titus 2:13; Hebrews 1:1ff., 8; 13:8; 1 John 1; 4:9; Revelation 1:8, 17; 22:13 in *C.D.*, I, 1, 459f. For a recent approach to Christology through the titles of Christ in Scripture see Oscar Cullmann, *The Christology of the New Testament*, Eng. tr. by S. C. Guthrie and C. A. M. Hall (S.C.M. Press, 1959, 1963²).

man,[8] and in this very act reveals God. And only God alone can do this. Therefore, Barth concludes, Christ's work in reconciliation and revelation *demands the acknowledgment that its Subject is identical with God in the full sense of the word*.[9] In Barthian terminology Jesus Christ is *the objective reality and possibility of revelation*.[1] In the more familiar language of the Fourth Gospel Jesus Christ is the way, the truth and the life, apart from whom no man comes to the Father.[2] If we have seen Him we have also seen the Father.[3] To be this, He must be God Himself.

Even when we have acknowledged this, we have not exhausted all that the New Testament has to say about revelation. To put it in Barth's language: 'Manifestation must be added as something special, as a special act of the Father or the Son or both, to the givenness of the revelation of the Father in the Son.'[4] It is this manifestation, this 'subjective side in the event of revelation'[5] which the New Testament represents as the work of God Himself in the person of the Holy Spirit. As a factor in revelation, the Spirit is

---

[8] See Barth's exegesis of Matthew 16:16; John 4:10; 6:35, 68 in *C.D.*, I, 1, p. 463; and Romans 5:11; 2 Corinthians 5:18ff.; Colossians 1:20ff.; Ephesians 2:14f.; 1 Timothy 2:5; Hebrews 9:15; 12:24 in *C.D.*, I, 1, pp. 468f.

[9] *C.D.*, I, 1, p. 470.   [1] *C.D.*, I, 2, pp. 1–44.

[2] John 14:6.   [3] John 14:9.

[4] *C.D.*, I, 1, p. 514. Empirical perception of the truth is necessary (1 John 1:1f.), but of itself it is incapable of revealing God. To perception must be added inward illumination (2 Corinthians 3:5; Matthew 16:17; Mark 4:11f.) which is the gift of the Father (Matthew 16:17; John 6:44ff., 65; 10:29; *cf.* John 1:12f.; 3:3; Revelation 22:1; Ephesians 1:8f.). (*Cf. C.D.*, I, 1, pp. 514f.)

[5] *C.D.*, I, 1, p. 515 where Barth bases his teaching on John 3:5; 20:22; Acts 2; 19:2f.; 1 Corinthians 12:3; 2:12; Romans 8:9; 2 Corinthians 3:6; Ephesians 1:13, 17. The Spirit guarantees to man participation in revelation (*C.D.*, I, 1, pp. 518f.; *cf.* Romans 5:5; 8:9ff.; 10:8; 1 Corinthians 2:10; 3:16; 6:19; 2 Corinthians 1:22; 5:5; 6:16; Ephesians 1:14; Hebrews 6:5; 1 John 4:13). He gives man instruction and guidance which he cannot give himself (*C.D.*, I, 1, pp. 519f.; *cf.* John 14:17, 26; 15:26; 16: 13; Acts 8:29; 10:19; 13:2; 16:6; Romans 8:14; 2 Corinthians 1:3f., 21; Galatians 5:18; 1 John 2:20). It is in virtue of the Spirit that human language can become testimony to the living God (*C.D.*, I, 1, pp. 520ff.; *cf.* Mark 13:11 and parallels; Luke 12:12; John 15:26; Acts 1:8; 22; 19:6; 1 Corinthians 12 and 14; 2 Corinthians 4:6). It is the Spirit that sets man free for the service of God (*C.D.*, I, 1, pp. 522f.; *cf.* John 8:31–59; Romans 8:21; 2 Corinthians 3:17; Galatians 5:1).

not 'a new instruction, illumination, stirring up of man proceeding beyond Christ, beyond the Word, but simply as the
instruction, illumination, stirring up of man by means of
the Word, on behalf of the Word'.[6] In this, too, the Spirit
exercises a Lordship which is both distinct from and yet
one with that of the Father and the Son.[7] In short, Barth
approaches the person of the Holy Spirit along the same
lines as he approached the person of Christ. 'The work of
the Holy Spirit in revelation is a work which can only be
ascribed to God Himself, and which is therefore and
expressly ascribed to God.'[8] But whereas Christ is *the objective reality and possibility of revelation*, the Spirit is *the
subjective reality and possibility of revelation*.[9]

c. Barth and the orthodox formulation of the doctrine of the Trinity

After centuries of wrangling and debate the early church
settled down to think of God as three *persons* in one *substance*. Although 100 per cent unanimity was never achieved,
it became the accepted practice to speak of the Father, the
Son and the Holy Spirit as three *persons* (Latin *personae*;
Greek ὑποστάσεις) and of the divine nature as one *substance* (Latin *substantia*; Greek οὐσία) or *essence* (Latin
essentia).[1] Thus the Council of Chalcedon of 451, which was
generally recognized by both the Catholic and Protestant
churches as having pronounced the definitive orthodox view
of Christ, could speak of Him as being 'of one substance with
the Father as regards His Godhead' and yet at the same time
as being 'one person'.[2] This way of speaking was taken over
by the Protestant churches at the time of the Reformation.
It appears for instance in the first of the Thirty-Nine Articles
of the Church of England:

---

[6] *C.D.*, I, 1, p. 518.
[7] See Barth's exegesis of John 1:33; 7:38f.; 14:16, 26; 15:26; 16:7, 13; 20:22;
Acts 2:2; 10:44; 11:15; 1 Corinthians 6:11; 12:4f.; 2 Corinthians 3:17; 13:14;
1 Peter 1:2 in *C.D.*, I, 1, pp. 516f.
[8] *C.D.*, I, 1, p. 534.   [9] *C.D.*, I, 2, pp. 203–279.
[1] For a brief history of the doctrine down to Barth and his contemporaries see
R. S. Franks, *The Doctrine of the Trinity* (Duckworth, 1953).
[2] Bettenson, p. 73.

> There is but one living and true God, everlasting, without body, parts, or passions; of infinite power, wisdom, and goodness; the Maker, and Preserver of all things both visible and invisible. And in unity of this Godhead there be three Persons, of one substance, power, and eternity; the Father, the Son, and the Holy Ghost.

This statement could easily be paralleled by excerpts from other Reformed[3] (and for that matter, Catholic[4]) pronouncements.

With this in mind we may approach Barth's formulation of the doctrine of the Trinity. He sums it up in this way:

> We mean by the doctrine of the Trinity . . . the proposition that He whom the Christian Church calls God and proclaims as God, therefore *the God who has revealed Himself according to the witness of Scripture, is the same in unimpaired unity, yet also the same in unimpaired variety thrice in a different way.* Or, in the phraseology of the dogma of the Trinity in the Church, *the Father, the Son and the Holy Spirit in the Bible's witness to revelation are the one God in the unity of their essence, and the one God in the Bible's witness to revelation is in the variety of His Persons the Father, the Son and the Holy Spirit.*[5]

This formulation, Barth admits, goes beyond Scripture in two ways:

> The Bible lacks the express declaration that the Father, the Son, and the Holy Spirit are of equal essence and therefore in an equal sense God Himself. And the other express declaration is also lacking, that God is God thus and only thus, i.e. as the Father, the Son, and the Holy Spirit. These two express declarations, which go beyond the witness of the Bible, are the twofold content of the Church doctrine of the Trinity.[6]

Nevertheless, Barth insists, both points are implicit in Scrip-

---

[3] The Article dates from 1553. It is drawn mainly from the First Article of the Lutheran Confession of Augsburg (1530) and the Thirteenth Article of the Concordat of 1538. *Cf.* also the Westminster Confession, II.

[4] *Cf.* Denzinger, Nos. 993ff., for views at the time of the Council of Trent.

[5] *C.D.*, I, 1, p. 353.   [6] *C.D.*, I, 1, p. 437.

ture. Moreover, it is necessary to make them in order to bring out the full implications of biblical teaching.

Having said this, it must also be said that whilst Barth subscribes to the teaching of Christian orthodoxy, he has his own ways of expressing it.

Barth defends the unity and equality of essence of the Trinity by insisting that:

> The name of Father, Son, and Spirit means that God is the one God in threefold repetition; and that in such a way, that this repetition itself is grounded in His Godhead; hence in such a way that it signifies no alteration in His Godhead; but also in such a way that only in this repetition is He the one God; in such a way that His Godhead stands or falls with the fact that in this repetition He is God; but precisely for the reason that in each repetition He is the one God.[7]

We may call each member of the Trinity a *person* and employ the modern concept of personality in the sense of an individual self-consciousness. But we must always add the rider that we are doing this to distinguish the divine *Thou* from an *it*, and that 'we are not speaking of three divine "I's", but thrice of the one divine "I" '.[8]

This great stress on the unity of God, coupled with Barth's peculiar way of speaking, could give the impression that Barth was serving up his own brand of the ancient mon-

---

[7] *C.D.*, I, 1, p. 402.

[8] *C.D.*, I, 1, p. 403. The unity of God in Barth's teaching is further characterized by his acceptance of the doctrine of *co-inherence* (*perichoresis*) and the rule: *opera trinitatis ad extra sunt indivisa*. The doctrine of *co-inherence* 'signifies at once the *confirmation* of the distinction between the modes of existence (none of them would be what it is – not even the Father! – apart from its co-existence with the others) and the *relativisation* of it (none of them exists as a special individual, all three "inexist" in one another, they exist only in common as modes of the existence of the one God and Lord who posits Himself from eternity to eternity)' (*C.D.*, I, 1, p. 425, where Barth cites John 10:30, 38; 14:10f.; 17:11 and the statements in Paul on the relationship between Christ and the Spirit. It was first formulated by John of Damascus, *Ekdosis*, I, viii and xiv). The rule that the works of the Trinity are indivisible in their operation which goes back to Augustine is described by Barth as 'the rule for theologising on the Trinity' (*C.D.*, I, 1, p. 430; *cf. On the Trinity*, I, iv; V, xiv).

archian heresy, teaching that three persons of the Trinity were merely temporary modes or manifestations of the single divine being. This impression might appear to be strengthened by Barth's desire to substitute the term *mode of being* (German *Seinsweise*) for the traditional term *person*.[9] But the impression would be superficial. The term *mode of being* is not intended to indicate something temporary, but rather to point to the ways in which God *is* both in revelation and in Himself. God does what He does and is what He is in revelation, because of what He is in Himself. The existence and nature of the *economic* Trinity revealed through Scripture depend upon the existence and nature of the *immanent* Trinity, *i.e.* upon God as He is in Himself. God the Father is revealed as the Father because He is so 'antecedently in Himself':[1]

> Because already beforehand, quite apart from the fact that He reveals Himself to us as such, He is what He reveals Himself as being, namely, the Father of Jesus Christ His Son, who as such is Himself God. He can be so, *because He is Himself the Father in Himself, because Fatherhood is an eternal mode of existence of the divine essence*.[2]

Similarly, the Son is eternally the Son of the Father, because:

[9] Barth qualifies his suggestion by pointing out that his proposed change is intended to be no more than '*relatively* better' than the customary term *person* (*C.D.*, I, 1, p. 412). The change is designed to guard against *Tritheism*. It also calls attention to the fact that when the term *person* was first applied to the members of the Trinity, those who used it did not start out with our modern conception of *person*. In his detailed review of the technical terminology Barth suggests that the meaning of ὑπόστασις in Hebrews 1:3 depicts the Son as 'an "impress", a countertype of the "Father's" mode of existence' (*ibid.*, p. 413). In line with this both Calvin and Aquinas thought of the divine persons as that which subsist within the being of God. Aquinas defined the divine persons as 'realities subsisting in the divine nature' (*Summa Theologiae*, I, QQ. 29, 30; *cf.*, *ibid.*, pp. 409f.). Calvin interpreted *person* as 'a subsistence in the being of God' (*Institutes of the Christian Religion*, I, xiii, 6; *cf. ibid.*, p. 413). Earlier still, Augustine had pointed out that the term *person* did not mean exactly the same when applied to God as when applied to men. It was used less for what it says positively than for its value as a safeguard against monarchianism (*On the Trinity*, V, ix; VII, iv; *cf. ibid.*, pp. 408f.). In short, Barth claims that his thought is in the main stream of orthodox interpretation. Conversely, the attempt to read back into the divine persons modern ideas of human personality is a comparatively recent innovation (*ibid.*, pp. 410f.).

[1] *C.D.*, I, 1, p. 441; *cf.* pp. 382, 548.
[2] *C.D.*, I, 1, p. 448.

Revelation has *eternal* content and *eternal* validity. Throughout all the depths of deity, not as the penultimate but as the ultimate thing to be said about God, God is God the Son just as He is God the Father.[3]

In the same way, Barth defends the Western Church's acceptance of the *filioque* clause in the Nicene-Constantinopolitan Creed. The procession of the Spirit from the Father and the Son is not limited to the giving of the Spirit in time at Pentecost, but expresses an eternal relationship within the being of God.[4]

Barth's doctrine of the Trinity represents the most imposing attempt in modern times to restate the orthodox doctrine of the Trinity. Above all, it is grounded upon God's revelation of Himself in Christ. It might be said that it is the supreme example of the underlying principle of Barth's thinking, that *all God's dealings with men are effected in and through the person of Jesus Christ.*[5] For the doctrine is essentially a development of the implications of revelation in Christ. All this was worked out in the *Prolegomena* of the *Church Dogmatics*, written in the pre-war years as a prelude to Barth's statement of the Christian message proper. Since then his thought has been by no means static. It has, in fact, taken a momentous (and, in the opinion of the present writer, retrograde) step in the rigorously Christological way it has proceeded to expound the Christian message. We shall consider this in our fourth chapter on 'Barth's Christ-centred Approach to God, Creation and Reconciliation'. In the meantime, we must consider an important corollary of his teaching on the Word of God – Barth's teaching on the bankruptcy of natural theology.

[3] *C.D.*, I, 1, p. 474.
[4] *C.D.*, I, 1, pp. 541–557. For further historical background to this question see J. N. D. Kelly, *Early Christian Creeds* (Longmans, 1950), pp. 358–367. The Latin term *filioque* (= 'and the Son') which now appears in the creeds of the Western church was not originally there. It was added perhaps first in the sixth century to the clause: 'the Holy Spirit Who proceedeth from the Father' thus making official the doctrine of *Double Procession, i.e.* that the Holy Spirit proceeds from the Son as well as from the Father. The doctrine remains a cause of division between the Western churches and the Eastern Orthodox churches who have never accepted the clause.
[5] See above, pp. 20, 35, 66f.

3 THE BANKRUPTCY OF NATURAL THEOLOGY

To hang a dog and yet still retain an air of respectability and fairness, it is first of all necessary to give it a bad name. In theological and religious circles this means that the most convenient way of disposing of some unwelcome person or argument is to label them as extreme or negative. Thus we are relieved of the necessity of taking the man seriously, however cogent his arguments may be.

To an unfortunately large extent this is what has happened to Karl Barth. Even at the present day Barth is known, one might almost say is notorious, in Anglo-Saxon theological circles for one particular facet of his teaching, and that a negative one – his repudiation of natural theology. The fact is doubly unfortunate, because it means that his positive contributions are largely by-passed and the cogency of his arguments against natural theology largely ignored.

By natural theology we mean the attempt to work out coherent doctrines of God and His relationships with men without recourse to the special revelation of Christ in the Gospel. It may proceed, as with Descartes or Spinoza, with the mind's attempt to prove the existence of God by speculative reason.[1] Or it may, with Thomas Aquinas,[2] attempt to argue back to some ultimate first cause on the basis of what we see in nature. Or it may adopt a more intuitive approach, as when Paul Tillich tries to convince the unbeliever that he believes in God already because he has

[1] René Descartes, *Discourse on Method*, 1637, IV; *Meditations on the First Philosophy*, 1641, III; Benedict Spinoza, *Ethics*, 1677, I.
[2] *Summa Theologiae*, I, Q. 2.

ultimate concerns which Tillich assures him is the same as believing in God.[3]

The aims and motives of a natural theology may be various. It may attempt to demonstrate the reasonability of belief in God and religious values as a prelude to accepting the Christian faith. Thus it might hope to establish some common ground between believer and unbeliever. But from here it is only a short step to using it as a tool for correcting the religion of faith by bringing it into line with the dictates of reason. And from here it is but another short step to abandoning revealed religion altogether in favour of some rational religion conceived in terms of a preconceived philosophy. Broadly speaking, Thomas Aquinas and Roman Catholic theology fall into the first category,[4] whilst Paul Tillich belongs to the last.[5]

Karl Barth rejects all this on two counts – two counts which are really complementary. On the one hand, God is sovereign and free. Knowledge of Him is a matter of grace. He has revealed Himself in Christ who is alone man's way back to God. On the other hand, these arguments are always in practice blind alleys. By themselves they never add up to encounter with the living God.

The purpose of this chapter is to examine Barth's grounds for saying this. The issue is of obvious importance both to those who are seeking God and to those concerned with the presentation of the Christian message. We shall approach the question from three angles. First (under the heading 1 *The Debate with Brunner*), we shall look at the celebrated controversy of the 1930s in which Emil Brunner accused Barth of overstating his case and pleaded for a new type of

[3] *Cf.* Tillich's sermon on 'The Depth of Existence' in *The Shaking of the Foundations* (1949, Pelican, 1963), especially pp. 63ff. *Cf.* Tillich's formal statement on the subject in his *Systematic Theology*, I (Nisbet, 1953).

[4] For a Roman Catholic critique of Barth's position see Hugo Meynell, *Grace Versus Nature: Studies in Karl Barth's Church Dogmatics* (Sheed and Ward, 1965).

[5] Although Tillich speaks of revelation, he does not do so in any Barthian or orthodox sense. Revelation is a matter of exploring the depths of reason where reason comes to the end of its capacities, bringing us into contact with *being itself* (*cf. Systematic Theology*, I, Pt. 1, 'Reason and Revelation', pp. 79–177; and the article by the present writer 'Tillich and his Critics' in the *Theological Students' Fellowship Bulletin*, No. 41, Spring 1965, pp. 3–7).

natural theology. The points at issue here might at first sight
strike the English reader as rather involved and not at all
the most obvious points to be made in a debate on natural
theology. But it has to be remembered that Brunner was
trying to pioneer a new type of natural theology which
would harmonize with a Protestant, evangelical approach to
the gospel. Moreover, the points debated did include the
central question of whether God reveals Himself in nature.
Secondly (under the heading II *Proofs of the Existence of
God*), we shall look at a subject which is still very much in
the air. Can we prove rationally and objectively that there
is a God? Finally (under the heading III *Natural Theology
and Revelation in Nature*), we shall return to the questions:
Does God reveal Himself in nature? And if so, is it possible
to build up some sort of a natural theology?

I THE DEBATE WITH BRUNNER

English students of theology are apt to bracket Barth and
Brunner together, as teaching more or less the same things,
the only difference being that Brunner takes rather less time
to say them. In point of fact, there has been a deep rift between the two for the past thirty years, and it shows little
sign of healing. The clash came in 1934, and it was Brunner
who fired the first shot with the publication of a paper entitled *Nature and Grace. A Contribution to the Discussion
with Karl Barth.*[6] Brunner adopted the stance of an admirer
of Barth's great work in resuscitating biblical theology and
changing the face of Protestantism. Thanks to Barth, things
were not what they used to be. Whereas liberalism spoke
vaguely about religion, theologians and ministers were
recovering a fresh vision of the Word of God.[7] But having
granted all that, Brunner asked whether Barth had not gone
too far. In particular, he listed six points at which Barth

---

[6] Brunner's paper and Barth's reply are published together in the Eng. tr. of
Peter Fraenkel in *Natural Theology; Comprising 'Nature and Grace' by Professor
Dr. Emil Brunner and the reply 'No!' by Dr. Karl Barth* (Bles, 1946). Page references
are to this edition. It contains an introduction by John Baillie who also
summarizes the debate in *Our Knowledge of God* (O.U.P., 1939 and many
reprints), pp. 3–43.
[7] *Op. cit.*, pp. 17f.

had overstated his case. If these points were seen in their proper light they would give us a pointer to the way a genuine natural theology could be developed. But if these points are to be denied in the way that Barth denies them it would mean the end of a Christian approach to ethics[8] and education.[9] Moreover, these points present a point of contact for the presentation of the Christian message.[1] Barth's reply appeared in the October of the same year. It bore the succinct title *No! Answer to Emil Brunner*.[2] For the sake of convenience, we shall consider Brunner's thesis and Barth's reply together in the order in which Brunner makes them.

a. The image of God
Brunner's first thesis concerns man as he is made in the image of God. He charges Barth with teaching that this image has been completely destroyed by sin:

> Since man is a sinner who can be saved only by grace, the image of God in which he was created is obliterated entirely, *i.e.* without remnant. Man's rational nature, his capacity for culture and his humanity, none of which can be denied, contain no traces or remnants whatever of that lost image of God.[3]

By contrast, Brunner thinks that this goes too far. He wishes to draw a distinction between the *formal* and *material* aspects of that image. The *formal* aspect is that which distinguishes man from beasts (*cf.* Genesis 1 : 26 and Psalm 8), viz, that man is a rational, responsible creature. The latter is bound up with the original righteousness which man had before he sinned. Whereas Brunner grants that this latter is 'completely lost' through sin, the former remains unaffected. Man is still a man, even though he is a sinner.[4] And this, Brunner thinks, presents a starting-point for natural theology.

All this might sound very impressive, but Barth asks what does it really prove. The contention that man's undestroyed *formal* likeness to God provides the objective possibility of

[8] *Op. cit.*, pp. 51f.   [9] *Op. cit.*, pp. 57f.   [1] *Op. cit.*, pp. 58ff.
[2] See above, p. 79, n. 6.   [3] *Op. cit.*, p. 20.   [4] *Op. cit.*, pp. 22ff.

revelation is quite beside the point. Brunner's talk about 'man's capacity for revelation' proves nothing about natural theology unless Brunner also means to say that man actually has some revelation of God already in him as part and parcel of that capacity. But Brunner does not. In short, Brunner's point is just as relevant as the fact that a man who has been saved from drowning is still a man and not a lump of lead. The fact that he is the former and not the latter makes no contribution whatever to his being saved.[5] Brunner's point is a red-herring. Nothing pertinent to the discussion can be drawn from it, because revelation comes to man from without. It is not something which man has already in his possession or which can be worked up from his own sinful, innate capacities.

In this reply Barth contented himself with exploiting Brunner's self-contradictions and *non-sequiturs*. A full exposition of what Barth means by the *image of God* was not to appear for another decade. When it did, it took a completely unexpected turning, without, however, taking Brunner's point.[6]

b. General revelation

In the second place, Brunner charged Barth with exalting revelation in Christ at the expense of revelation in nature. He proceeded to put into Barth's mouth the following thesis:

> Since we acknowledge scriptural revelation as the sole norm of our knowledge of God and the sole source of our salvation, every attempt to assert a 'general revelation' of God in nature, in the conscience and in history, is to be rejected outright. There is no sense in acknowledging two kinds of revelation, one general and one special. There is only one kind, namely the one complete revelation in Christ.[7]

Against this Brunner asserts that revelation in Christ and revelation in nature are not mutually contradictory. Indeed, God 'leaves the imprint of his nature upon what he does'.[8]

---

[5] *Op. cit.*, pp. 79f.
[6] *C.D.*, III, 1, pp. 183ff.; see below, pp. 112f.
[7] *Op. cit.*, p. 20.   [8] *Op. cit.*, p. 25.

Pointing out Barth's failure to treat this question seriously in his *Epistle to the Romans* when Paul treats it in Romans 1 and 2, Brunner concludes:

> The reason why men are without excuse is that they will not know the God who so clearly manifests himself to them.[9]

Later on Barth was to repair this omission and give more careful consideration to such passages as Psalm 19 : 1f.; Acts 14; 17 and Romans 1 : 19ff.[1] But in *No!* his energies were devoted to exploiting the contradictions in Brunner's case. Brunner wants to say that the world is 'somehow recognisable' to man as the creation of God, and also that 'sin makes man *blind* for what is visibly set before us'.[2] He cannot have it both ways.

We shall look at the question and Barth's later views more closely at the end of this chapter. Suffice it to say for the present that although there are certain isolated instances where biblical writers speak of revelation in nature, none of them entertains the possibility of erecting a complete theology upon it. In each case the emphasis falls upon man being reminded of his responsibility towards God through the works of nature.

c. Preserving grace

Brunner's third thesis accuses Barth of so exalting saving grace that he utterly denies that grace is at work in the creation and preservation of the universe. He sums up Barth's teaching like this:

> Accordingly we have to draw the following conclusion from the acknowledgment of Christ as the sole saving grace of God: there is no grace of creation and preservation active from the creation of the world and apparent to us in God's preservation of the world. For otherwise we would have to acknowledge two or even three kinds of

[9] *Op. cit.*, p. 25; *cf.* p. 61.
[1] *Cf. C.D.*, II, 1, pp. 119ff.; *A Shorter Commentary on Romans*, pp. 26ff. See below, pp. 94–98.
[2] *Op. cit.*, p. 80; *cf.* pp. 24f.

grace, and this would contradict the oneness of the grace of Christ.[3]

Against this, Brunner propounds his own thesis that there is such a thing as preserving grace, distinct from saving grace, which does not abolish sin but only the worst consequences of it. For whenever the concepts of an omnipotent, loving God and sin are taken seriously, a third notion arises – that of God's gracious preservation. And again this provides a starting-point for natural theology.

Barth's reply is particularly interesting in the light of his subsequent thought. He insists that there are not two kinds of grace but one – the one saving grace of Christ, revealed in the gospel. All that Brunner refers to as preserving grace is really an aspect of saving grace:

> We have time, because Christ ever intercedes for us before the judgment-seat of God . . . Does not the Bible relate all that Brunner calls a special 'preserving grace' to prophecy and fulfilment, to law and gospel, to the covenant and the Messiah, to Israel and to the Church, to the children of God and their future redemption? Where did Brunner read of another abstract preserving grace?[4]

Taken by itself, this preserving grace which Brunner defends 'might just as well be our condemnation to a kind of antechamber of hell!'[5] These criticisms contain within them the seeds of the universalism which Barth fights against in his later teaching,[6] but which is implicit in the way he understands the central thesis of his theology: that all God's dealings with men are effected in and through the person of Christ.[7] His criticism of Brunner at this point stands or falls with his view of grace, the latter being revealed only in the gospel. But apart from that it may well be asked what coherent theology may be deduced merely from our experiences of life.

---

[3] *Op. cit.*, pp. 20f.; *cf.* pp. 27ff.   [4] *Op. cit.*, pp. 83f.
[5] *Op. cit.*, p. 84.   [6] See below, pp. 130–133.
[7] See above, pp. 20, 31, 35, 76, and below, pp. 103–108, 124–126.

d. *The divine ordinances*

Brunner's fourth point is really an extension of his third. It concerns Barth's denial that we can see the hand of God in certain divine ordinances. He accuses Barth of teaching that:

> Accordingly there is no such thing as God's ordinances of preservation, which we could know to be such and in which we could recognise the will of God which is normative for our own action. A *lex naturae* of this kind which is derived from creation can be introduced into Christian theology only *per nefas*, as a pagan thought.[8]

By contrast, Brunner sees marriage, the essential nature of which remains uncorrupted by the fall, as an *ordinance of creation*, and the state, the function of which is to check sin, as an *ordinance of preservation*.[9] And again this provides a basis for a Christian natural theology.

In reply, Barth grants the existence of certain moral and social axioms, but asks: 'Do instinct and reason really tell us what is *the* form of matrimony, which would then have to be acknowledged and proclaimed as a divine ordinance of creation?'[1] On Brunner's premises, the laws of biology and chemistry have greater claim to be called ordinances of creation, since they are clearer and more certain.[2]

e. *Point of contact*

In the fifth place, Barth is said to deny that the grace of Christ finds any ready-made point of contact in man:

> For the same reason it is not permissible to speak of the 'point of contact' for the saving action of God. For this would contradict the sole activity of the saving grace of Christ, which is the centre of the theology of the Bible and the Reformation.[3]

Once more Brunner thinks that this goes too far. His own view again falls back on his distinction between the *formal* and *material* aspects of the image of God. Man's intelligence

---

[8] *Op. cit.*, p. 21.   [9] *Op. cit.*, pp. 29ff.   [1] *Op. cit.*, p. 86.
[2] *Ibid.*   [3] *Op. cit.*, p. 21.

and sense of responsibility (the *formal* aspect of the image
of God) provide a natural point of contact. The possibility
of man being addressed at all by the Word of God depends
upon his capacity to receive words and his sense of responsibility. This, Brunner assures Barth, in no way jeopardizes
the uniqueness of Christ as the sole source of grace. But without this point of contact revelation of the Word is unthink-
able.[4]

Again in his reply Barth launches a swashbuckling attack
on Brunner's self-contradictions.[5] But like Brunner's point,
it really retraces the old ground covered under the first
thesis. To be of any use at all in the construction of a
natural theology Brunner has to show what, in fact, he
admits cannot be shown: that the *formal* aspect of the
image of God carries in it a prior knowledge of God. Otherwise the point is irrelevant to the establishment of a natural
theology.

f. Whether grace abolishes or perfects nature

Brunner's sixth and last thesis accuses Barth of over-exalting
grace at the expense of nature. It alleges that on Barth's
view, regenerating grace dissolves and replaces our former
natures:

> Similarly the new creation is in no wise a perfection of
> the old, but comes into being exclusively through destruc-
> tion of the old and is a replacement of the old man by
> the new. The sentence, *gratia non tollit naturam sed per-
> ficit*, is in no sense correct, but is altogether an arch
> heresy.[6]

Brunner, however, holds that this Latin phrase – that
grace does not abolish nature but perfects it – enshrines an
important truth which is bound up with natural theology.
In his defence of the point he again resorts to his distinction
between the *formal* and *material* aspects of the divine image
in man, and asks what happens when a man becomes a
Christian. Conversion does not abolish our human natures;

[4] *Op. cit.*, pp. 31ff.   [5] *Op. cit.*, pp. 87–90.
[6] *Op. cit.*, p. 21; *cf.* Aquinas, *Summa Theologiae*, I, Q. 1, art. 8, ad 2.

it changes something that is already there. As a case in point
Brunner looks at Galatians 2 : 20. When Paul speaks of the
death of the old nature and of Christ living in him, he does
not mean that his human personality is abolished. The
death of the old nature described in Galatians 2 : 20 refers to
the *material* aspect only. The *formal* aspect remains. It is
ridiculous, he argues, to say 'the Holy Spirit within me has
faith'.[7] The nearest the Bible comes to such a statement is
1 Corinthians 2 : 10–12 which he paraphrases: 'In so far as
we have the Holy Spirit, there takes place in us an act of
divine self-consciousness through the Holy Spirit.'[8] But this
does not mean that our personalities are destroyed by grace.
Faith is not mysticism, and to believe does not make a man
identical with Christ.

But far from dealing the death-blow to Barth's position,
Brunner's argument has again missed the point.[9] To establish his case for a natural theology, Brunner would have
to show that the passages he adduces above presuppose a
natural knowledge and affinity with God as the prerequisite
for new life in Christ. But, as Barth proceeds to show, 1
Corinthians 2 : 14 indicates that this knowledge is a gift of
the Holy Spirit beyond the comprehension of the natural
man. As in Galatians 2 : 20, the old nature is not so much
a bridge between the natural man and God as a barrier to
be broken down. In conclusion, Barth points out, the main
stress of the passages in question together with that of 2
Corinthians 5 falls neither on the abolition nor reparation
of human nature but on the *miracle* performed on man by
grace in making him a new creature. In this light, Brunner's
talk about the *formal* aptitude of the image of God in man
is *uninteresting*, and any *material* aptitude is *impossible*.[1]

At this point the two contestants proceeded to debate the
theology of the Reformers to see what part, if any, natural
theology played in their teaching.[2] The discussion was
interesting and informed, but is of less significance for the
present study.

As we look at the two essays side by side, there can be
little doubt as to who really won the day. Brunner was, as

[7] *Op. cit.*, p. 33.   [8] *Op. cit.*, p. 34.   [9] *Op. cit.*, pp. 90–94.
[1] *Op. cit.*, p. 94.   [2] *Op. cit.*, pp. 35–50, 94–109.

ever, lucid and persuasive. But when subjected to rigorous
scrutiny his case evaporated. This was not least due to his
own vagueness of purpose. Nowhere in his essay did he
really outline the sort of natural theology he envisaged. It
fell between two stools. It wanted to retain the Reformed
emphasis on salvation by grace and faith alone, and also
say that man could know something about God by nature.
Barth insisted that the two ideas cancelled each other out.
For real knowledge of God is the work of God's grace. Barth
did not seriously entertain the idea of a knowledge of God
which was not a saving knowledge. Brunner failed to make
out a case for a natural theology that could stand up by
itself. On his own premises he hankered after but could not
establish a natural theology in any valid sense of the term.[3]
Consequently, Barth had little difficulty in shooting him
down simply by exploiting the ambiguities of his position.
But what Brunner did show, even if it was not his chief
aim, was that no theology can afford to neglect the theology
of nature. And this was where Barth was inclined to overstate his case.

It must be remembered that Barth was at that time still
in the later phases of the process of sloughing his Dialectical
Theology. He did not really do justice to Brunner's point
about revelation in nature. The conclusions that he drew
were valid in the light of the biblical teaching on the knowledge of God. Natural theology in the sense that he defines
it[4] is a blind alley incapable of leading to a coherent, detailed knowledge of God. But the route he took to get to this
conclusion short-circuited an important strand of biblical
teaching and area of human experience. It must also be

[3] The reader of Brunner's essay has great difficulty in making out what
Brunner really has in mind apart from joining issue with Barth on the points
we have examined. Apart from general talk about clearing away obstacles
and the value of the image of God Brunner has no constructive programme
(*cf. op. cit.*, pp. 58f.).

[4] 'By "natural theology" I mean every (positive *or* negative) *formulation of a
system* which claims to be theological, i.e. to interpret divine revelation, whose
subject, however, differs fundamentally from the revelation in Jesus Christ and
whose *method* therefore differs equally from the exposition of Holy Scripture'
(*op. cit.*, pp. 74f.). Barth goes on to say that such a theology does not really
exist. It is a pseudo subject (*ibid.*, p. 75).

remembered that this was not Barth's (or for that matter
Brunner's[5]) last word on the subject. In the final section of
this chapter we shall try to see how Barth sought to repair
his omissions at this point. But before doing so, it is worth
while taking a glance at the so-called proofs of the existence
of God.

II PROOFS OF THE EXISTENCE OF GOD

Neither Barth nor Brunner will have anything to do with
the so-called proofs of the existence of God.[6] Logically and
theologically they are fully justified in taking this attitude.
At best these point to one who is not the living God of faith,
but to some abstract *first cause, absolute* or *necessary being.*
As such, they are more of a rival than a stepping-stone to
Christian faith in the triune God.

a. The cosmological and teleological arguments

The cosmological argument seeks to argue back to an
ultimate first cause. Put in its most basic terms, it argues
that every event must have a cause. Nothing causes itself.
Therefore, if we press back far enough we must come up
against a first cause. The teleological argument applies a
similar process of reasoning, only it thinks in terms of design
and purpose rather than causation, arguing back to a great
purposive mind behind the universe.[7]

---

[5] Brunner published a second much enlarged version of his essay in 1935, but
graciously allowed the first version to be translated in the Eng. tr. so that it
would match Barth's (*op. cit.,* pp. 7f.). Brunner returned to the subject at
various points in *Revelation and Reason: The Christian Doctrine of Faith and Knowledge,* Eng. tr. by Olive Wyon (S.C.M. Press, 1947), and *The Christian
Doctrine of God, Dogmatics,* I, Eng. tr. by Olive Wyon (Lutterworth, 1949,
1958[3]).

[6] *Cf. C.D.,* II, 1, pp. 4ff., 305ff.; *C.D.,* III, 1, pp. 5ff.; Emil Brunner, *Revelation and Reason,* pp. 338–348; *The Christian Doctrine of God,* pp. 149f.

[7] Perhaps the classical statement of these arguments appears in Thomas
Aquinas, *Summa Theologiae,* I, Q. 2, which may be compared with Kant's
classical refutation in his *Critique of Pure Reason,* Transcendental Dialectic –
Book II, ch. iii. For modern restatements see E. L. Mascall, *He Who Is: A
Study in Traditional Theism* (Longmans, 1943), pp. 30–82; F. Copleston, *A
History of Philosophy,* Vol. II, *Mediaeval Philosophy: Augustine to Scotus* (Burns &
Oates, 1950, 1954), pp. 336–346; Edward Sillem, *Ways of Thinking about God:
Thomas Aquinas and Some Recent Problems* (Darton, Longman and Todd, 1961).

Such arguments tend to raise more problems than they solve. Quite apart from Kant's objection that they contain implicitly the untenable ontological argument, there is the problem of demonstrating that the first cause is the same as the great designer and that both are the same as the Christian God. Logically, we are not entitled to attribute to a cause any capacities other than those implied by the effect. If, for the purposes of argument, we grant that there is a first cause, the proof does not entitle us to say that he is the same as the great designer. It is one thing to make something, it is something else to design it. The more proofs we have of this kind, the more the difficulty is intensified. The difficulty reaches its climax when we try to identify these different 'gods' which we accept on the basis of our reason with the Christian God whom we believe in with our faith. It is true that Christians believe that their God is both the ultimate cause of things and also their designer, but this is an article of faith.[8] Why should we abandon the 'gods' of reason for the God of faith? Indeed, we can do so only on the basis of an act of faith. In other words, so far as offering rational proof for the Christian God is concerned, we are back to square one.

But this is not the only difficulty. The 'gods' posited by the proofs are not the living God encountered in experience. They are hypotheses, posited by arguments. They may be known by their effects. They are not known directly in everyday life. They are no more than hypotheses, designed to explain certain given situations.

It is no accident that those who have most strenuously advocated such proofs have been those who have found it necessary to reinterpret and modify biblical faith to make it fit their philosophical notions of religion. But in point of fact, the logic of these proofs is more than suspect. For the conclusion (that there must be an uncaused cause or an un-designed designer) denies one of the argument's initial premises (that nothing can cause or design itself). What the arguments really point to is a regress of causes which disappear from the grasp of the human mind in the mists of infinity.

[8] *Cf.* Hebrews 11:3.

It is sometimes suggested that such proofs do not actually prove the Christian God, but that they help us towards such a belief. But in rational argument a miss is as good as a mile. Two or three invalid arguments do not add up to one valid one. All they do is to add up to two or three invalid arguments.

It may be said that people have been helped by such proofs in the past, and therefore we ought not to despise them. In reply it should be pointed out that it is perfectly possible to believe the right thing for the wrong reason, but that for the sake of the integrity of the Christian message and the security of the foundations of a man's faith, to employ dubious arguments – however well intentioned – is both fraudulent and dangerous.

The same applies, Barth argues, to the practice of trying to prove the doctrine of the Trinity by detecting all manner of threefold relationships in nature or even divine triads in various non-Christian religions.[9] Barth acidly comments: 'If all that crops up as a triadic godhead merits the appellation "God", then the history of religion is a confirmation of the Christian Trinity; but not otherwise. For what is left over after deducting the question of the nature there described as the nature of God, is really only the number three.'[1]

b. The ontological argument

Of a somewhat different order is the ontological argument first formulated by Anselm in the eleventh century. This is usually conceived as an attempt to deduce the existence of

---

[9] The idea that God has left imprints of the Trinity (*vestigia trinitatis*) on His creation goes back to Augustine (*On the Trinity*, VI, 10; IX–XI; *Confessions*, XIII, 11f.; *The City of God*, XI, 24f.). Originally they were perhaps no more than illustrations. But from the idea of an illustration it is but a short step to treating them as some kind of proof. This line of approach has continued in Reformed theology down to modern times. For example, H. Bavinck found such imprints of the Trinity in nature, culture, history, religion and psychology (*Gereformierde Dogmatiek*, II, 1918, pp. 332f.). On all this see *C.D.*, I, 1, pp. 383–399. Barth rejects these analogies because they never turn out to be real analogies of the Trinity.

[1] *C.D.*, I, 1, p. 393.

God from the idea of the most perfect being.[2] There must be some most perfect being. For if this were merely an idea of the mind and did not actually exist, it would not be the most perfect being. Modern philosophical objections are undoubtedly sound which reject the argument on the grounds that existence cannot be treated as a predicate and that reality cannot be discovered merely by taking thought independently of all observation.[3]

Barth, however, has cogently argued in his *Anselm: Fides Quaerens Intellectum*,[4] that this was not Anselm's point at all. What Anselm was attempting to do was not to try to derive God's existence merely from a concept of God, but to show that we cannot rationally deny the living God once we know who He is.[5] In other words, his argument is not

[2] Classical discussions of the argument appear in Anselm, *Proslogion*, ii–iv; Descartes, *Meditations*, V; Leibniz, *Monadology*, xlv. It was rejected by Gaunilo in his *Liber pro Insipiente* and by Aquinas and Kant in the course of their discussions of the existence of God in the passages cited from their works on p. 88, n. 7.

[3] On this see Ninian Smart, *Historical Selections in the Philosophy of Religion* (S.C.M. Press, 1962), pp. 57f. (who gives a text but unfortunately not the relevant context of Anselm's argument). There are two chief objections to the argument. On the one hand, existence is not one quality alongside others which an object may or may not have and yet still continue to be. It either exists or it does not exist at all. G. E. Moore brought out the difference between existence and qualities or properties by comparing the two sentences: 'Some tame tigers do not growl' and 'Some tame tigers do not exist'. The ontological argument, as commonly understood, treats existence as a property alongside others which constitute the perfections of the most perfect being. The other line of thought argues that definitions do not tell us anything about reality, unless they are confirmed by observation. But the argument tries to prove its point from pure thought.

[4] See above, pp. 21f., 47–54.

[5] Barth rightly points out that the traditional way of stating the argument ignores both its context and Anselm's theological method generally. Anselm's thought is characterized by the axiom: *Credo ut intelligam* (I believe that I may understand) (*op. cit.*, pp. 22–26). As he says in *Proslogion*, i: 'If I did not believe, I would not understand.' The same applies to his *Cur deus homo*. When Anselm speaks of finding 'necessary reasons' for the incarnation 'apart from Christ', he does not mean that he is looking for them outside the Christian. Rather it is like finding an unknown *x* on the basis of the other truths that are already known within the orbit of the faith such as the fact of sin, man's need of a redeemer, the love of God, *etc.* (*op. cit.*, p. 55). Anselm's argument itself seeks to answer the question how it is that the fool can say in his heart that there is no God (Psalms 14:1; 53:1; *cf. ibid.*, pp. 105f.). Anselm is not

a piece of natural theology at all, but an understanding of
the implications of the Christian revelation.

c. Revelation – the ultimate proof

Later on in the *Church Dogmatics* Barth acknowledged that
it was from Anselm that he had learned his 'fundamental
attitude to the problem of the knowledge and existence of
God'.[6] It is not a question of whether God *can* be known.
We must start from the fact that God *is* actually known and
will be known again from His Word.

> Where God is known He is also in some way or other
> knowable. Where the actuality exists there is also the
> corresponding possibility. The question cannot then be
> posed *in abstracto* but only *in concreto*; not *a priori* but
> only *a posteriori*. The *in abstracto* and *a priori* question
> of the possibility of the knowledge of God obviously pre-
> supposes the existence of a place outside the knowledge
> of God itself from which this knowledge can be judged. It
> presupposes a place where, no doubt, the possibility of
> knowledge in general and then of the knowledge of God
> in particular can be judged and decided in one way or
> another. It presupposes the existence of a theory of know-
> ledge as a hinterland where consideration of the truth,
> worth and competence of the Word of God, on which the
> knowledge of God is grounded, can for a time at least be
> suspended. But this is the very thing which, from the
> point of view of its possibility, must not happen. Just as
> the reality of the Word of God in Jesus Christ bears its
> possibility within itself, as does also the reality of the Holy

---

concerned with a hypothetical God but with the God known in the Christian
faith. The concept of God as *That than which no greater can be thought* (*Proslogion*, ii) is based upon faith. Anselm draws the distinction between an idea
and that which the idea represents. What the fool denies is the former. We
cannot deny the latter, once we grasp what God is. Anselm concludes:
'No one who understands what God is can think that God does not exist, even
though he may say these words in his heart' (*Proslogion*, iv; *cf. op. cit.*, pp.
161–171). Barth's work is a brilliant phrase-by-phrase discussion of Anselm's
Latin text. For further discussion see John McIntyre, *St. Anselm and his
Critics: A Re-interpretation of the Cur Deus Homo* (Oliver and Boyd, 1954), pp.
7–55.

[6] *C.D.*, II, 1, p. 4.

Spirit, by whom the Word of God comes to man, so too
the possibility of the knowledge of God and therefore the
knowability of God cannot be questioned *in vacuo*, or by
means of a general criterion of knowledge delimiting the
knowledge of God from without, but only from within
this real knowledge itself. Therefore, it is quite impossible
to ask whether God is knowable, because this question is
already decided by the only legitimate and meaningful
questioning which arises in this connexion.[7]

The only scientifically legitimate path to the knowledge
of God is to start with the way God has revealed Himself.
It does not need a ready-made religious point of contact. It
brings its own. Like the Word in Ezekiel's vision of the
valley of the dry bones in Ezekiel 37, it brings its own
illuminating, life-bringing power. It is fatuous to object with
Tillich that this is unacceptable to the modern, thinking
man who is wrestling with doubt.[8] In other scientific and
academic disciplines we cannot shape the evidence to what
we think it ought to be before we can accept it. The path
to knowledge is shaped by the evidence. The nature of the
discipline is dictated by the object of its study. The same is
true in the realm of theology. Indeed, modern man has
doubts about the truth of religion precisely because the type
of evidence that he wants does not exist and because he
refuses to look seriously at the real evidence that does exist.

As a footnote to all this, it is ironical to note that if we
compare Barth's writings with those of Paul Tillich, it is
Barth and not Tillich who gets more closely to grips with
modern thought and culture. Whereas Tillich talks vaguely
and generally, Barth in the small-print passages of the
Church Dogmatics carries on a continuous dialogue in much
detail with the great thinkers of the past and present. Barth's
rejection of natural theology is not a rejection of culture[9]
and the creation. Both have their proper place. Barth's point

[7] *C.D.*, II, 1, p. 5.
[8] *Ultimate Concern: Tillich in Dialogue*, edited by D. Mackenzie Brown (S.C.M.
Press, 1965), pp. 189f.
[9] On the place of the arts and Barth's great passion for Mozart see his paper
'Wolfgang Amadeus Mozart', reprinted in *Religion and Culture: Essays in
Honor of Paul Tillich*, edited by Walter Leibrecht (S.C.M. Press, 1958), pp.
61–78.

is that we do justice to neither the true source of knowledge of God nor the creation if we exalt the latter to fulfil a function of the former.

III NATURAL THEOLOGY AND REVELATION IN NATURE

In discussing Barth's debate with Brunner, it was suggested that Barth rode roughshod over an important biblical strand of teaching and a correspondingly important area of human experience by failing to do justice to revelation in nature.[1] Many people who are not Christians profess an awareness of the deity. And many people who are Christians admit to a general awareness of God before they came to a full Christian faith. Whilst confirming what the Psalmist and Paul say in Psalm 19: 1f.; Acts 14: 17; 17: 22–31; Romans 1: 19ff., 32; 2: 12–16, this would seem both to undermine Barth's principle that God reveals Himself only through His Word and also leave the door open for natural theology.

In his earlier writings Barth seems to resort to the expedients either of flatly denying the implications or of ignoring these passages altogether. But his later writings are relevant to understanding their significance.

Barth now acknowledges that there is an objective revelation of God in nature. Commenting on Romans 1 : 19ff., Barth writes:

> The world has always been around them, has always been God's work and as such God's witness to Himself. Objectively the Gentiles have always had the opportunity of knowing God, His invisible being, His eternal power and godhead.[2]

But Paul can hardly mean to teach in Romans what he denies in 1 Corinthians 2 : 6–16, where he speaks

> of that hidden wisdom of God, which eye has not seen and ear has not heard, which does not enter into the heart

[1] See above, pp. 81f., 87f. The most extensive recent treatment of this subject is G. C. Berkouwer's *General Revelation* (Eerdmans, Grand Rapids, 1955). It takes Barth's earlier views as its starting-point, and includes a detailed survey of Roman Catholic and biblical teaching.

[2] *A Shorter Commentary on Romans*, p. 28; *cf. C.D.*, I, 2, pp. 306f.; *C.D.*, II, 1, pp. 119ff.

of any man, which the natural man does not accept, which he cannot apprehend, which only the Spirit of God can know and which man can only know through this Spirit of God.[3]

And in fact, he makes it plain that he does not. Far from using this awareness of God's eternal power and deity as a bridge to God and an occasion for true worship, man in his sin has used it as a barricade against God. Instead of honouring God, man has opted to worship gods of his own making. And this in turn has backfired on his moral life. Although he is aware of the heinousness of sin, his heart is set on it.[4] The inference that Paul draws from all this is not that man can work out a true, coherent theology based upon rational reflection on the constitution of the universe. In practice, man does not. Indeed, he cannot have any intimate knowledge of God apart from the gospel. For, as the rest of Romans goes on to show, real knowledge of God is not a matter of acquiring certain factual information, but of being united with Christ and having one's life transformed. Paul's purpose in Romans 1 and 2 is simply to demonstrate

that Gentiles and Jews stand before God without excuse, fully answerable and responsible for their opposition to Him (1 : 20; 2 : 1).[5]

Barth interprets Psalm 19 and Acts 17 in similar vein. Although the heavens declare the glory of God, they do not set out a complete theology. The opening verses of the Psalm should be read in the light of what follows. It is the law of the Lord which, being perfect, revives the soul, and His commandments which enlighten the eyes (Psalm 19 : 7f.). And this is in line with the main thrust of Old Testament teaching.[6] In examining Paul's Areopagus speech in Acts 17 and the speech at Lystra in Acts 14 : 15–17, Barth rightly

[3] *A Shorter Commentary on Romans*, p. 27.
[4] Romans 1 :32.
[5] *Op. cit.*, p. 28. Barth goes on to point out that the seriousness of sin becomes fully apparent only in the gospel in so far as it takes Christ's death to reveal how serious it is.
[6] *C.D.*, II, 1, pp. 101f.

draws attention to what positive results this revelation in nature produces. They were in fact non-existent. Had the Athenians really known God, they would not have erected an altar 'To an unknown God'. There may have been a dim awareness. But it needs Paul to proclaim to them what they worship as unknown (Acts 17 : 23).[7]

Nor does Romans 2 : 12–16 teach anything fundamentally different. Paul, Barth argues,[8] is not concerned with a hypothetical response of the heathen who fulfils the spirit of the law without ever having heard it. In saying this, Barth is well aware that he is parting company with the majority of exegetes of this passage. Nevertheless, his reasons for doing so are weighty. Barth claims that Paul is talking about none other than the Gentile converts, who, though they did not have the law, nevertheless have received the Spirit which has so changed their lives that they show that the law is written upon their hearts. This latter is a direct fulfilment of the prophecy of the new covenant made in Jeremiah 31 : 31ff. Certainly, this explanation fits the context of Paul's argument in the light of what Paul has already said about heathen religion in chapter 1 and what he goes on to say about having the externals of the law in chapters 2–4, and the necessity of being led by the Spirit in chapter 8. It also fits missionary experience.[9]

Thus, if we look at these passages in context, none of them offers any encouragement to anyone looking around for a biblical precedent for erecting a natural theology. But the questions may be asked: What is the scope of this knowledge of God in nature, and how does it come to us? The most specific of these passages is Romans 1 : 20 which says: 'Ever since the creation of the world his invisible nature, namely,

---

[7] C.D., II, 1, pp. 121ff.; C.D., I, 2, pp. 304ff.

[8] C.D., I, 2, p. 304; C.D., II, 2, pp. 242, 604; C.D., IV, 1, pp. 33, 369, 395.

[9] Perhaps the most serious objection to Barth's exegesis turns around the meaning of the word *nature* ($\phi\acute{\nu}\sigma\iota\varsigma$) in 2:14. But in the light of Romans 2:27; 11:21ff.; 1 Corinthians 11:14f.; Galatians 2:15; 4:8; Ephesians 2:3, *nature* cannot simply be equated with some metaphysical, super-personal principle which exists over against God. Rather it denotes the way in which a thing or person exists, his *disposition*. Such a meaning would be quite compatible with Barth's interpretation. On this question see J. B. Soucek, '*Zur Exegese von Röm. 2:14ff.*' in *Antwort*, pp. 99–113.

his eternal power and deity, has been clearly perceived in the things that have been made. So they are without excuse.' The text together with Romans 1 : 32 indicates that this knowledge is still operative. Whilst commentators acknowledge this, they generally appear reluctant to say how this knowledge works. Aquinas takes the passage as his cue for unfolding his arguments for the existence of God.[1] He can hardly be right. Paul speaks of a direct knowledge mediated by the works of creation which is there for all and sundry to see. Aquinas speaks of what is really a hypothetical explanation at the end of a chain of reasoning which only the relatively intelligent and sophisticated can follow. As a tentative answer to our question, it might be suggested that what Paul has in mind is a knowledge which works in a way parallel to that mediated by the Word and the sacraments. In neither of the latter cases is this knowledge an inference back from the material words or elements. Rather it is given in and through them. They remain what they are, yet the divine presence accompanies them. Paul would seem to be saying that in the act of living in the world we are profoundly aware that God is the author of the things around us, that their excellence demonstrates His excellence, and that this is constant proof of our responsibility to God.

This knowledge does not give us leave to speculate. It is confined to His 'eternal power and deity'. The revelation of the gospel shows how little we do know. But in neither case – revelation in nature and revelation through the Word – is knowledge of God separable from experience of God. It is not possible to construct a theology like a two-storey building, the first floor being laid by reason and the top floor built by faith. To make any progress at all, reason and faith must go together from first to last. Reason plays its part in discerning and apprehending what is revealed.[2] But this in turn calls for the response of faith in acknowledging responsibility to God, repentance in turning away from sin and trust in self-commitment. It is only as this process continues that a real theology – in the proper sense of the word as knowledge of God – emerges.

[1] *Summa Theologiae*, I, Q. 2, art. 2.
[2] *Cf. C.D.*, IV, 3, pp. 848ff.

One final point. Does this revelation of God in nature undermine Barth's teaching that Christ is the sole mediator of revelation and the underlying principle that all God's dealings with men are effected in and through Christ? Again we must be cautious. The biblical writers give no direct answer to this question. But there are passages which speak of the Word or the Son as the agent of creation and providence.[3] And if we take these together with the passages already noted which testify to the Son as the mediator of revelation, then the answer suggested is that the revelation of God in nature is also a revelation of the Son.[4]

[3] John 1:3f.; Colossians 1:16; Hebrews 1:2f.

[4] Whether or not men actually follow this light, this appears to be the natural way of taking John 1:9 (cf. 1:10ff.; 8:12ff.). But see also C. K. Barrett, *The Gospel According to St. John: An Introduction with Commentary and Notes on the Greek Text* (S.P.C.K., 1955), pp. 134f. It should be further noted that Barth insists that this revelation of God in nature should be viewed in the context of the covenant of grace in Christ (cf. *C.D.*, II, 1, pp. 112ff.). It is in virtue of this covenant, Barth argues, that the creation came into being (cf. below, pp. 110–113). For further discussion of the existence of God in modern theology see H. Gollwitzer, *The Existence of God as Confessed by Faith*, Eng. tr. by J. W. Leitch (S.C.M. Press, 1965); see also John Hick, *The Existence of God, Readings Selected, Edited, and Furnished with an Introductory Essay* (Macmillan, 1964).

4 BARTH'S CHRIST-CENTRED APPROACH TO GOD, CREATION AND RECONCILIATION

Like all great thinkers, Karl Barth is a man who is not afraid to change his mind. Over the years he has found it necessary to write no less than three quite different commentaries on Romans. He scrapped the first version of his *Christian Dogmatics* and entirely rewrote it as the first volume of his *Church Dogmatics*. Barth has changed from the liberalism of Harnack and Herrmann to Dialectical Theology, and from Dialectical Theology to his own neo-orthodox doctrine of the Word of God. But even within the *Church Dogmatics* a change of emphasis has taken place which is scarcely less profound than the earlier changes. It could be described as a shift of emphasis from the revealing Word of God to the Word of God incarnate.[1] Whereas, in the first volume of the *Church Dogmatics* Barth is concerned with the revelation of what man could not know apart from the Word of God, in the later volumes Barth takes the incarnation of that Word as the key to all theological truth. For reasons that will be made clear later on, it seems to the present writer that the way Barth has worked this out is a retrograde step. But it is a logical development of the principle which seems to underlie Barth's thought since his first commentary on Romans: that all God's dealings with men are effected in and through the person of Jesus Christ. Moreover, since God is sovereign, loving and gracious, the whole of man's destiny is affected by the love and grace revealed in Jesus Christ.

In this chapter we shall try to assess Barth's approach to the incarnation and its effect on three major doctrines: his doctrines of God, creation and reconciliation.

[1] *Cf.* Hans Urs von Balthasar, *op. cit.*, p. 124.

I THE INCARNATION, THE COVENANT AND GOD

Barth's new emphasis began to make its presence really felt
in the second part of the second volume of the *Church
Dogmatics* which dealt with *The Doctrine of God*, and
which was completed in 1942. Early on in the first chapter
Barth makes this significant statement:

> Jesus Christ is indeed God in His movement towards man,
> or, more exactly, in His movement towards the people
> represented in the one man Jesus of Nazareth, in His
> covenant with this people, in His being and activity
> amongst and towards this people. Jesus Christ is the de-
> cision of God in favour of this attitude or relation. He is
> Himself the relation. It is a relation *ad extra*, un-
> doubtedly; for both the man and the people represented
> in Him are creatures and not God. But it is a relation
> which is irrevocable, so that once God has willed to enter
> into it, and has in fact entered into it, He could not be
> God without it. It is a relation in which God is self-
> determined, so that the determination belongs no less to
> Him than all that He is in and for Himself. Without the
> Son sitting at the right hand of the Father, God would
> not be God. But the Son is not only very God. He is also
> called Jesus of Nazareth. He is also very man, and as such
> He is the Representative of the people which in Him and
> through Him is united as He is with God, being with Him
> the object of the divine movement. That we know God
> and have God only in Jesus Christ means that we can
> know Him and have Him only with the man Jesus of
> Nazareth and with the people which He represents. Apart
> from this man and apart from this people God would be
> a different, an alien God. According to the Christian per-
> ception He would not be God at all. According to the
> Christian perception the true God is what He is only in
> this movement, in the movement towards this man, and
> in Him and through Him towards other men in their
> unity as His people.[2]

A page later he adds:

> Everything happens according to this basic and determina-
> tive pattern, model and system. Everything which comes

[2] *C.D.*, II, 2, p. 7.

from God takes place 'in Jesus Christ', i.e. in the establishment of the covenant which, in the union of His Son with Jesus of Nazareth, God has instituted and maintains and directs between Himself and His people, the people consisting of those who belong to Him, who have become His in this One. The primal history which underlies and is the goal of the whole history of His relationship *ad extra*, with the creation and man in general, is the history of this covenant. The primal history, and with it the covenant, are, then, the attitude and relation in which by virtue of the decision of His free love God wills to be and is God. And this relation cannot be separated from the Christian conception of God as such.[3]

What we have here is the key to Barth's understanding of God which in turn provides the key to his understanding of every other doctrine. Perhaps we can draw out the significance of these statements by spotlighting three important facets of Barth's thought.

a. The covenant
More than once in these two passages Barth uses the term 'covenant'. He does so in his own special sense. The term is, of course, a biblical one. It denotes the special relationships, solemnly ratified by sacrifice,[4] between God and Israel in the first instance and then between God and the church.[5] The

---

[3] *C.D.*, II, 2, pp. 8f.

[4] *Cf.* Genesis 15:17f.; Exodus 24:8; Matthew 26:28; Mark 14:24; Luke 22:20; 1 Corinthians 11:25; Hebrews 9:20; 10:29.

[5] The Old Testament mentions various covenants between men (*e.g.*, Genesis 21:27, 32; 26:28). But the idea of God's covenants with His people could be described as the central theme of biblical religion. God made a covenant with Noah (Genesis 9:9–17) never again to flood the earth. The idea of the constitution of the people of God through the covenant begins with Abraham (Genesis 15; 17). It was established again with Moses (Exodus 24; but *cf.* 2:24; 6:4ff.). Although there is no record of the making of a covenant with David, it would seem that God made one with him (Psalm 89:3f., 26ff.; *cf.* 2 Samuel 7:12–17). This latter was ultimately messianic in its reference (Isaiah 42:1, 6; 49:8; 55:3f.; Malachi 3:1; Luke 1:32f.; Acts 2:30–36). The covenant was renewed under Josiah (2 Kings 23) and Ezra and Nehemiah (Nehemiah 9–10). But already the Old Testament looks forward to a new covenant, wider in scope and greater in blessing (Jeremiah 31:31ff.; *cf.* Ezekiel 36:26ff.; 37:14; Hebrews 8:8–12; 10:16f.; Luke 1:67–79). Jesus saw His death as the means of instituting this new covenant (Matthew 26:28;

central idea was the promise that God would be their God
and that they should be His people.[6] As such, it forms the
backbone of biblical religion and Reformed theology. Barth
takes this idea up, but extends it to include not only believers
but mankind in general.

It is significant that Barth offers no biblical exegesis at
this point to support his case. (That is, none apart from
the irrelevant passing mention of Colossians 2:9 and
Colossians 1:19.)[7] But his logic is clear. The essential idea of
the covenants is the union or partnership of God and man.
The focal point of all is the union of the Son of God with
Jesus of Nazareth. Thus in view of the union of divine and
human nature in the incarnation, Barth posits a union of
God with mankind generally. For, as his teaching goes on to
imply, Christ's human nature embraces all humanity. The
history of this relationship is the *primal history* which underlies all history. It is universal history in microcosm. Everything that happens, happens *according to this basic and
determinative pattern, model and system*. Whatever one
might say about this, and we shall have a good deal to say
about it and its implications later on,[8] at least it must be
said that Barth has carried through his programme that all
God's dealings with men are effected in and through the
person of Jesus Christ.

Mark 14:24; Luke 22:20; 1 Corinthians 11:25; Hebrews 10:29). Its scope
now included the Gentiles. For a brief summary of the biblical position see
John Murray, *The Covenant of Grace: A Biblico-Theological Study* (Tyndale
Press, 1954); and the articles by John Murray in *The New Bible Dictionary*, ed.
J. Douglas (I.V.F., 1962), pp. 264–268; G. E. Mendenhall in *The Interpreter's
Dictionary of the Bible*, ed. G. A. Buttrick (Abingdon; New York and Nash-
ville, 1962), I, pp. 714–723. The significance of the covenant was particularly
recognized in Post-Reformation theology, *cf.* H. Heppe, *op. cit.*, pp. 281–447.
Recent Old Testament studies of the covenant include W. Eichrodt, *Theology
of the Old Testament*, I, Eng. tr. by J. A. Baker (S.C.M. Press, 1961) and R. E.
Clements, *Prophecy and Covenant* (S.C.M. Press, 1965).

[6] Exodus 6:7; Leviticus 26:12; Jeremiah 7:23; 11:4; 30:22; 31:33; 32:38;
2 Corinthians 6:10; Hebrews 8:10; Revelation 21:3.

[7] *C.D.*, II, 2, pp. 5 and 7. Barth comments on the significance of the title
Emmanuel (= God with us) in Matthew 1:21f.; Isaiah 7:14 in *C.D.*, IV, 1,
pp. 5f. But his detailed exegesis does not appear until *C.D.*, IV, 1, pp. 22–34,
and then it does not establish his point.

[8] See below, pp. 103–139.

b. Election

Barth unfolds this conception of the covenant in the context of his teaching on election. Again Barth is drawing upon an idea which figures prominently in both Scripture and the Reformers.[9] But again he applies it in a significantly different way.[1] Whereas for the Reformers and the biblical writers the election of some to salvation implied the non-election of others, for Barth the election of the man Jesus means the election of all mankind. Jesus Christ is both the God who elects and the man who is elected. This leads to the further difference that, whereas Calvin postponed his exposition of election and predestination almost to the end of his teaching on grace in his *Institutes*, Barth puts it at the very forefront of his teaching. He regards it as 'the sum of the Gospel' and places it at the very heart of his teaching on the doctrine of God.[2]

> The doctrine of election is the sum of the Gospel because of all words that can be said or heard it is the best: that God elects man; that God is for man too the One who loves in freedom. It is grounded in the knowledge of Jesus Christ because He is both the electing God and elected man in One. It is part of the doctrine of God because

[9] In Scripture election is first seen in connection with the choice of Abraham and his posterity, but even within the elect nation not all are equally chosen (Genesis 12:1-7; 17:1-14; 21:12f.; 25:21ff.; Deuteronomy 4:37ff.; 7:6ff.; Malachi 1:2f.; Romans 9; Galatians 4:21-31). The Reformers based their teaching on God's grace shown in the election of individuals to salvation on such passages as Matthew 11:27; 13:11; John 1:12f.; 6:37ff., 44f.; 10:27ff.; 13:8; 15:19; 17:6, 9, 11f., 19ff., 24; Romans 8:28ff.; 9:1-11:36; Ephesians 1:4-12; 2:1-10; Titus 1:1; 1 Peter 2:4-10. For the Reformers' teaching see Article XVII of the Thirty-Nine Articles of the Church of England; Martin Luther, *On The Bondage of the Will: A New Translation of De Servo Arbitrio (1525) Martin Luther's Reply to Erasmus of Rotterdam*, translated by J. I. Packer and O. R. Johnston (James Clarke, 1957); Calvin, *Institutes of the Christian Religion*, III, xxi-xxiv; *Concerning the Eternal Predestination of God*, translated and edited by J. K. S. Reid (James Clarke, 1961) (It is interesting to compare Calvin's teaching in this work with the somewhat Barthian introduction of the editor); H. Heppe, *op. cit.*, pp. 150-189; Philip Edgcumbe Hughes, *Theology of the English Reformers* (Hodder, 1965), *passim*. For a modern restatement of the practical implications of this teaching see J. I. Packer, *Evangelism and the Sovereignty of God* (I.V.F., 1961).

[1] For Barth's own observations on this see *C.D.*, II, 2, p. x.

[2] *C.D.*, II, 2, pp. 3-506 on 'The Election of God'.

originally God's election of man is a predestination not merely of man but of Himself. Its function is to bear basic testimony to eternal, free and unchanging grace as the beginning of all the ways and works of God.[3]

What Barth still has in common with the Reformers is his stress on sovereign grace. There is nothing in man as man to make God inclined to choose him and save him. From first to last man's salvation is entirely a work of grace. There remains too the same language. But apart from this, the whole pattern has been transformed. What has changed it is the way Barth has rearranged it to fit the thesis that all God's dealings with men are effected in and through the person of Jesus Christ. He has become both the electing God and the elected man.[4]

(i) *Jesus Christ as the electing God.* To the Reformers election and predestination were mysteries in the deepest sense of the word. They acknowledged them as facts of Scripture and experience, before which man could only bow in submissive wonder.[5] Behind them stood God's absolute and

---

[3] *C.D.*, II, 2, p. 3.
[4] On this see especially the section on 'Jesus Christ, Electing and Elected' in *C.D.*, II, 2, pp. 94–145.
[5] *Cf.* Luther's comment: 'Keep in view three lights: the light of nature, the light of grace, and the light of glory . . . By the light of nature, it is inexplicable that it should be just for the good to be afflicted and the bad to prosper; but the light of grace explains it. By the light of grace, it is inexplicable how God can damn him who by his own strength can do nothing but sin and become guilty. Both the light of nature and the light of grace here insist that the fault lies not with the wretchedness of man, but in the injustice of God; nor can they judge otherwise of a God who crowns the ungodly freely, without merit, and does not crown, but damns another, who is perhaps less, and certainly not more, ungodly. But the light of glory insists otherwise, and will one day reveal God, to whom alone belongs a judgment whose justice is incomprehensible, as a God whose justice is most righteous and evident – provided only that in the meanwhile we *believe* it, as we are instructed and encouraged to do by the example of the light of grace explaining what was a puzzle of the same order to the light of nature' (*op. cit.*, p. 317; *cf.* Calvin, *Institutes*, III, xxi, 1). Thus, the Reformers were not trying to work out a neat logical system. They were doing the opposite. They were acknowledging antinomies which were grounded in revelation but beyond the explanation of the human mind.

inscrutable decree, which was implied in the teaching of
Jesus Himself. Thus, Calvin commented on John 6 : 37, 39:
'The elect are said to have been with the Father before he
gave them to his only begotten Son.'[6] Barth denies this.
Whereas the Reformers held that God had revealed only
such things as God in His wisdom and love deemed fitting,
Barth holds that in Christ *all* His purposes are revealed.
On the basis of his understanding of the *covenant*, he there-
fore rejects any idea of an absolute decree and any election
apart from the election of mankind in Christ.

> We must not ask concerning any other but Him. In no
> depth of the Godhead shall we encounter any other but
> Him. There is no such thing as Godhead in itself. God-
> head is always the Godhead of the Father, the Son and the
> Holy Spirit. But the Father is the Father of Jesus Christ
> and the Holy Spirit is the Spirit of the Father and the
> Spirit of Jesus Christ. There is no such thing as a
> *decretum absolutum*. There is no such thing as a will of
> God apart from the will of Jesus Christ. Thus Jesus
> Christ is not only the *manifestatio* and the *speculum*
> *nostrae praedestinationis*.[7] And He is this not simply in the
> sense that our election can be known to us and contem-
> plated by us only through His election, as an election
> which, like His and with His, is made (or not made) by a
> secret and hidden will of God. On the contrary, Jesus
> Christ reveals to us an election which is made by Him, by
> His will which is also the will of God. He tells us that He
> Himself is the One who elects us.[8]

Whilst he acknowledges the pastoral prudence of the
Reformers in seeking to turn men's eyes away from gloomy
introspection and speculation by pointing them to the love
of God revealed in the gospel,[9] Barth complains that their
teaching nevertheless means that men have to reckon with a

---

[6] *Institutes*, III, xxii, 7; *cf. C.D.*, II, 2, p. 67.
[7] Commenting on Ephesians 1 :4, Calvin uses this phrase, calling Christ a *mirror*
in which we may contemplate our own election (*Institutes*, III, xxiv, 5). But he
does so in the sense rejected here by Barth.
[8] *C.D.*, II, 2, p. 115.
[9] *C.D.*, II, 2, pp. 65ff.

'blank', and 'unknown quantity' lurking behind the gospel. He also claims positive exegetical support for his view in the New Testament, where he finds such statements as 'All mine are thine' (John 17: 10) and 'The Father is greater than I' (John 14 : 28) balanced by 'and thine are mine' (John 17: 10) and 'the Father loves the Son, and has given all things into his hand' (John 3: 35). But when scrutinized, Barth's exegetical data do not substantiate his case. For whilst the Johannine understanding of the Father–Son relationship (upon which his case is chiefly based) traces the action of election concretely through the Son, it also points (as the Reformers insisted) to the prior decision of the Father.[1]

(ii) *Jesus Christ the elected man*. In propounding the complementary thesis that 'Jesus Christ is elected man',[2] Barth finds himself once more compelled to venture beyond the teaching of the Reformers. Once more he appears to take this step not in the interests of biblical exegesis but in working out the axiom that all God's dealings with men are realized in and through the person of Jesus Christ.

> In the predestination of the man Jesus we see what predestination is always and everywhere – the acceptance and reception of man only by the free grace of God. Even in the man Jesus there is indeed no merit, no prior self-sufficient goodness, which can precede His election to divine sonship. Neither prayer nor the life of faith can command or compel His election. It is by the work of the Word of God, by the Holy Spirit, that He is conceived and born without sin, that He is what He is, the Son of God; by grace alone. And as He became Christ, so we become Christians. As He became our Head, so we become His body and members. As He became the object of our faith, so we become believers in Him. What we have to

---

1 Of the relevant texts cited in *C.D.*, II, 2, pp. 106f., 110f., the following attribute election concretely to Jesus: John 13:18; 14:10; 15:16, 19; Matthew 11:27. They do not, however, rule out the possibility that Jesus calls whom He calls in accordance with the Father's will. The following by themselves could be understood in either the Barthian or the Reformers' sense: John 3:35; 5:26; 14:1, 6; 15:1f., 5; 17:1–5, 10. But the following support the Reformed interpretation, attributing election to a prior decision of the Father which is realized concretely through the Son: Matthew 16:17; John 6:37, 45, 65; 17:6, 9, 24; Ephesians 1:4.

2 *C.D.*, II, 2, p. 116.

consider in the elected man Jesus is, then, the destiny of human nature, its exaltation to fellowship with God, and the manner of its participation in this exaltation by the free grace of God. But more, it is in this man that the exaltation itself is revealed and proclaimed. For with His decree concerning this man, God decreed too that this man should be the cause and instrument of our exaltation.[3]

The operative words are contained in the last three sentences. On this basis Barth proceeds to teach a doctrine of double predestination, more radical (if less biblical) than anything the Reformers knew. Jesus Christ is at once elect for all and reprobate for all. But we shall have to look at this a little more closely later on, when we consider Barth's Christological approach to reconciliation.[4] Before leaving Barth's doctrine of the election of all in the election of the man Jesus Christ it is important to notice how flimsy is the exegetical support for this momentous doctrine.[5] Barth seeks it primarily in 'the basic passage', John 1 : 1f., which, he claims, 'contains self-evidently' the assertion 'that Jesus Christ is elected man'. But the assertion is anything but self-evident. In fact, it would seem to be wholly lacking in these verses. There is reference to the eternal love of the Father for the Son in John 17 : 24 and to the Chosen One in Luke 9 : 35; 23 : 35. But none of these passages provide the missing link in Barth's argument that the New Testament writers envisaged the election of mankind in general as comprehended in the particular election of the one man Jesus. Nor is this missing link supplied by the passages Barth cites which testify to the redemptive sufferings of Christ (Isaiah 42 : 1f.; 49 : 8; 53 : 9f.; John 19 : 5; Acts 2 : 23; 4 : 27f.; 1 Peter 1 : 20; Hebrews 2 : 11f.; 9 : 14; Revelation 13 : 8). Whilst these latter certainly speak of Christ as representing His people in His death and passion, and show that this people includes Gentiles, none of these passages conclusively shows that the election and representation of all mankind is implicit in the mission of Christ. The same applies when Barth proceeds to his two massive sections on 'The Election of the Community'[6]

[3] *C.D.*, II, 2, p. 118. [4] *C.D.*, II, 2, pp. 306–505. Note especially pp. 351–354. See also below, pp. 124ff., 131f.
[5] On this see *C.D.*, II, 2, pp. 117f. [6] *C.D.*, II, 2, pp. 195–30

and 'The Election of the Individual'.[7] Whilst there is much
of interest and insight in Barth's exposition of certain
passages of Scripture and the great theologians of the past,
exegetical evidence which would make Christ 'the all-
inclusive election'[8] is wanting.

Conversely, it may be pointed out that when the New
Testament writers speak of election, they have in mind a
definite body of people. The elect are those who show that
they are elect by their response to the gospel. They are either
those who have actually responded already in repentance
and faith or those who will do so in response to the Christian
message.[9]

c. The humanity of God

Finally, it should be remembered that all this is for Karl
Barth part of the doctrine of God. It is this which makes
God the sort of God that He is. God would not be God with-
out the *covenant*, without electing man to be His covenant
partner. Therefore Barth speaks of the *humanity of God*.[1]
When he does so, it is not in any general, altruistic sense.
Barth does not simply mean that God is concerned for man,
that He has man's best interests at heart. Rather, God has
taken humanity into a permanent relationship with Himself.
God's Godness 'includes in itself His humanity':[2]

> God shows and reveals who He is and what He is in His
> Godness, not in the vacuum of a divine self-sufficiency, but
> genuinely just in this fact that He exists, speaks and acts
> as partner (without doubt the absolutely superior partner)
> of man.[3]

All this is based, of course, upon Barth's idea of the *covenant* effected by the incarnation in view of the union of

---

[7] *C.D.*, II, 2, pp. 306–506.   [8] *C.D.*, II, 2, p. 117.

[9] *Cf.* (*e.g.*) Matthew 11:27–30; 22:14; John 1:12f.; 5:21–24; 6:35–40; 15:16;
17:6, 9, 20; Romans 8:29ff.; 9:11; 11:5; Ephesians 1:4f., 9, 11; 2:1; 2
Thessalonians 2:13; 2 Timothy 1:9; 2:19; 1 Peter 1:2; 2:4, 9.

[1] See Barth's paper on 'The Humanity of God', delivered at a meeting of
Swiss Reformed ministers in 1956 and reprinted in *God, Grace and Gospel*,
translated by J. S. McNab (Oliver and Boyd, 1959) (*S.J.T. Occasional Papers
No. 8*).

[2] *Op. cit.*, p. 41; *cf.* p. 37.   [3] *Op. cit.*, p. 37.

divine and human nature in the person of Jesus Christ. But this, in turn, involves a further idea. Humanity is taken up into the Godhead itself. The Second Person of the Trinity is no bare, discarnate Word. He is no *Logos asarkos*. The incarnation effected an indissoluble bond which is projected back into the very being of God, so that (Barth claims) the New Testament speaks of 'the One who in the eternal sight of God has already taken upon Himself our human nature'.[4] Thus, when once a student asked Barth whether the incarnation made a change in the Trinity, Barth replied:

> No, the incarnation makes no change in the Trinity. In the *eternal decree* of God, Christ is God and man. Do not ever think of the second Person of the Trinity as only *Logos*. That is the mistake of Emil Brunner. There is no *Logos asarkos*, but only *ensarkos*. Brunner thinks of a *Logos asarkos*, and I think this is the reason for his natural theology. The *Logos* becomes an abstract principle. Since there is only and always a *Logos ensarkos*, there is no change in the Trinity, as if a fourth member comes in after the incarnation.[5]

The connection here with natural theology is interesting. It might have been thought that Barth's own teaching would provide the thin end of the wedge for a natural theology.[6] Instead, he tries to turn the argument and accuse his opponents of natural theology by claiming that this is a revealed doctrine and that the idea of a *Logos asarkos* is itself a piece of rationalistic speculation.[7] But if we ask whether Barth's view is really grounded in the revelation witnessed to by Scripture, the answer must be in the negative. Whatever might be said about the human nature of Christ after the resurrection and ascension on the basis of

---

[4] *C.D.*, III, 1, p. 54.

[5] *Karl Barth's Table Talk*, recorded and edited by John D. Godsey (Oliver and Boyd, 1963) (*S.J.T. Occasional Papers No. 10*), p. 49.

[6] *Cf.* above, pp. 79–88, 98.

[7] 'We must not . . . imagine a "Logos in itself" . . . Like Godhead abstracted from its revelation and acts, it would necessarily be an empty concept which we would then, of course, feel obliged to fill with all kinds of contents of our own arbitrary invention. Under the title of a λόγος ἄσαρκος we pay homage to a *Deus absconditus* and therefore to some image of God which we have made for ourselves' (*C.D.*, IV, 1, p. 52).

such passages as Matthew 26:64; Acts 2:33–36 (*cf.* Psalm
110:1); 5:31; Romans 8:31; 1 Corinthians 15:20–28; Ephesians 1:20ff.; Hebrews 4:14; 7:24f.; 8:1–6; 9:11–28; 1 Peter
3:22 and 1 John 3:2, the New Testament does not project
the incarnation back into the being of God before the event
took place. And certainly the New Testament doctrines of
God do not envisage a general union of God and man as
part of the doctrine of God. Barth's attempts to prove the
contrary always fall short of their goal.[8] Ultimately the idea
is bound up with Barth's notion of the *covenant*. But however dubious the latter might be from the viewpoint of
biblical exegesis, there can be no question of its importance
for Barth. His whole approach to creation and reconciliation
is determined by this view of God and *covenant*.

II THE INCARNATION, THE COVENANT AND CREATION
As with Barth's doctrine of God it is again impossible to
examine every aspect of his teaching. We shall try to keep
in focus simply the main thrust of his teaching as it appears
under the three aspects of creation and covenant, man, and
evil.

a. Creation and covenant
In view of all that we have seen so far, it is not surprising
that Barth begins his account of creation first by insisting
that the doctrine of creation is a revealed doctrine,[9] and
then by insisting that creation must be viewed in the light
of the *covenant*.[1]

(*i*) *The Genesis creation narratives.* The central part of
Barth's opening volume on creation is taken up with a
massive exposition of the two creation narratives of Genesis
in terms of creation and covenant. The former (Genesis
1:1 – 2:4a) depicts 'Creation as the External Basis of the

---

[8] More than once Barth attempts to identify the subject of John 1:2 with the
incarnate Christ (*cf. C.D.*, II, 2, p. 117; *C.D.*, III, 1, p. 54). But this interpretation, though Barth deems it basic, seems hardly tenable. It is not
warranted by the verse itself, and would seem to make John 1:14 an irrelevant
tautology. Barth's exegesis of Hebrews 1:2f. and Colossians 1:15f. in *C.D.*,
III, 1, pp. 53f. is equally suspect.

[9] *C.D.*, III, 1, pp. 3–41.   [1] *C.D.*, III, 1, pp. 42–329.

Covenant'.[2] The latter (Genesis 2:4b–25) regards 'The Covenant as the Internal Basis of Creation'.[3] By means of this word-play Barth seeks to convey the theological symmetry of grace. Creation and *covenant* are not two separate realms. Both belong to the realm of grace. But neither are they identical. The first creation narrative shows how creation makes the *covenant* 'technically possible':

> Creation is not itself the covenant. The existence and being of the loved one are not identical with the fact that it is loved . . . The existence and being of the creature willed and constituted by God are the object and to that extent the presupposition of His love. Thus the covenant is the goal of creation and creation the way to the covenant. . . . The inner basis of the covenant is simply the free love of God, or more precisely the eternal covenant which God has decreed in Himself as the covenant of the Father with His Son as the Lord and bearer of human nature, and to that extent the representative of all creation. Creation is the external – and only the external – basis of the covenant. It can be said that it makes it technically possible; that it prepares and establishes the sphere in which the institution and history of the covenant takes place; that it makes possible the subject which is to be God's partner in this history, in short the nature which the grace of God is to adopt and to which it is to turn in this history.[4]

The second narrative, Barth claims, shows not only

> how creation promises, proclaims and prophesies the covenant, but how it prefigures and to that extent anticipates it without being identical with it; not only how creation prepares the covenant, but how in doing so it is itself already a unique sign of the covenant and a true sacrament; not Jesus Christ as the goal, but Jesus Christ as the beginning (the beginning just because He is the goal) of creation.[5]

Hence, in this sacramental scheme of reality, known only by faith, the creation of the firmament (Genesis 1:6ff.) depicts

[2] *C.D.*, III, 1, pp. 94–228. [3] *C.D.*, III, 1, pp. 228–329.
[4] *C.D.*, III, 1, p. 97. [5] *C.D.*, III, 1, p. 232.

not merely the physical separation of the waters, but the metaphysical creation of a barrier against chaos.[6] In the same way, the separation of light from darkness, of dry land from the sea, of day from night reflects the relationship between God's grace and His wrath.[7] This typological exposition reaches its climax with the creation of man. Turning his back upon everything he had previously written about the *image of God* in man being lost through sin,[8] Barth now expounds that image in terms of the mutual relationship of man and woman which reflects the mutual relationship that exists within the Godhead. The image of God expresses an *analogy of relationship*. Referring to the plural of the subject in Genesis 1:26 ('Let us make man in our image, after our likeness'), Barth observes:

> The relationship between the summoning I in God's being and the summoned divine Thou is reflected both in the relationship of God to the man whom He has created, and also in the relationship between the I and the Thou, between male and female, in human existence itself.[9]

The fact that the image is expressed in bi-sexuality corresponding to that of the animal kingdom belongs to creatureliness rather than to divine likeness.[1] The full significance of this relationship only comes to light in Barth's exposition of the relevant New Testament passages from which he deduces that Christ and His people together form the prototype of the image of God which is projected back into the creation.

> When the Old Testament gives dignity to the sexual relationship, it has in view its prototype, the divine likeness of man as male and female which in the plan and election of God is primarily the relationship between Jesus Christ and His Church, secondarily the relationship between Yahweh and Israel , and only finally – although very directly in view of its origin – the relationship between the sexes. It is because Jesus Christ and His Church are the internal basis of creation, and because Jesus Christ is

[6] *C.D.*, III, 1, p. 134.   [7] *C.D.*, III, 1, p. 142.
[8] See above, pp. 8of.   [9] *C.D.*, III, 1, p. 196.   [1] *Ibid.*

again the basis of the election and call of Israel, that the relation between Yahweh and Israel can and must be described as an erotic relationship.[2]

But if creation is sacramental, it is also historical. For all created reality is orientated around the history of salvation. This helps to explain why Barth is anxious to claim Genesis as saga and not myth. For myth, according to Barth, expresses certain recurrent, general relationships, clothed in the form of an apparently historical narrative, whereas saga records history, though expressed in the form of a tale with symbolic features.[3]

(ii) Christ and Adam: the covenant of grace and the covenant of works. The incarnation of Christ is thus no mere expedient, no mere *ad hoc* counter-measure, devised by the Father to deal with the problem of sin. God purposed from all eternity to take man into partnership with Himself in view of the covenant. But in order to make this possible, God had to make man. And in order to give man living space, God had to create the world. Thus 'the meaning of creation is to make possible the history of God's covenant with man which has its beginning, its centre and its culmination in Jesus Christ. The history of this covenant is as much the goal of creation as creation itself is the beginning

[2] *C.D.*, III, 1, p. 322. Here Barth expounds Genesis 2:18f. in the light of Ephesians 5:26f., *cf.* also *C.D.*, III, 1, pp. 201ff. It is evident from such passages as Genesis 9:6; Romans 8:29; 1 Corinthians 11:7; 2 Corinthians 3:18; 4:4; Colossians 1:15; 3:10 that the biblical writers do not regard the image of God in man as being totally destroyed by sin. On the other hand, it is not unmarred by sin. It is part of Christ's redemptive work to restore it. Whilst Genesis 1:26 does suggest that the image involves mutual relationship, 1 Corinthians 11:7 seems to preclude strict identification of the image with the male–female relationship. And the other New Testament passages referred to above identify the image in its strictest sense with Christ and not Christ plus His church or the man and wife relationship. For a critique of Barth's position see J. J. Stamm, '*Die Imago-Lehre von Karl Barth und die Alttestamentliche Wissenschaft*' in *Antwort*, 84–98. The most recent large-scale survey of the doctrine, which includes a consideration of Barth's teaching, appears in G. C. Berkouwer, *Man: The Image of God*, Eng. tr. by Dirk W. Jellema (Eerdmans, Grand Rapids, 1962). See also D. Cairns, *The Image of God in Man* (S.C.M. Press, 1953), who traces the history of thought on the subject from biblical times down to Barth and present-day views of man.
[3] *C.D.*, III, 1, pp. 81ff.; but *cf.* Klaas Runia, *op. cit.*, pp. 100ff.

of this history'.[4] From here it is but a small step to the equa-
tion: 'Adam is already Jesus Christ and Jesus Christ is
already Adam.'[5] For Christ is the ground and goal of everything, the focal point of humanity, the only one on whom
hinges the fate of mankind.

Barth's denial of a historical Adam arises not so much
out of anthropological or any other scientific considerations.
It is a theological necessity within his Christocentric system.
He brings this out himself in passing in the course of his
exposition of reconciliation when he contrasts his view of
the one *covenant of grace* with the older Reformed view of
the *covenant of grace* and the *covenant of works*.[6] This latter
was also known as the *covenant of nature*[7] and even the
legal covenant.[8] Although Barth's Reformed forbears were
well aware that none of these terms as such appeared in
Scripture and that Scripture does not record the formal conclusion of such a covenant, they coined these terms to give
expression to a relationship between man and God which
they did find in Scripture. It was designed to describe man
in his obligations towards his Maker. It was derived from a
study of such passages as Genesis 3; Leviticus 18: 5; Nehemiah
9: 29; Ezekiel 20: 11, 13, 20; Hosea 6:7; Luke 10: 28;
Romans 5: 12–21; 7: 10; 10: 5; Galatians 3: 12, and indeed
the whole biblical conception of man under the law.
Heidegger summed it up as follows:

> The covenant of works is God's pact with Adam in his
> integrity, as the head of the whole human race, by which
> God requiring of man the perfect obedience of the law of
> works promised him if obedient eternal life in heaven, but
> threatened him if he transgressed with eternal death; and
> on his part man promised perfect obedience to God's
> requirement.[9]

[4] *C.D.*, III, 1, p. 42.   [5] *C.D.*, III, 1, p. 203.

[6] *C.D.*, IV, 1, pp. 59ff. For the term and its significance see J. H. Heidegger,
Corpus Theologiae, 1700, IX, xv; H. Witsius, *De Oeconomia Foederum Dei cum
hominibus libri quattuor*, 1693³, I, ii, 1; (*cf.* H. Heppe, *op. cit.*, p. 283);
Westminster Confession, 1647, VII.

[7] J. Cocceius, *Summa Doctrinae de Foedere et Testamento Dei*, 1648, II, xxii (*cf.*
H. Heppe, *op. cit.*, p. 284).

[8] Raphael Egli, *De Foedere Gratiae*, II, xii (*cf.* Heppe, *op. cit.*, p. 285).

[9] J. H. Heidegger, *op. cit.*, IX, xv (*cf.* Heppe, *op. cit.*, p. 283).

The underlying premises of the doctrine are that Adam was a historical person, that before the fall he had a capacity to obey God perfectly, and that all men are somehow bound up with Adam in corporate solidarity as the head of the human race. Complementary to the *covenant of works* was the *covenant of grace* which was made with Christ and those who belong to Him.[1] It is this one covenant of grace which underlies the various covenants in the Old and New Testaments, for all these hold out the gift of life to those who are penitent and turn to God in faith.

Whilst Barth accepts the idea of corporate solidarity, he rejects the reasoning behind the older view. For him it posits two principles in God's action, the one for man as he is in Adam and the other for man as he is in Christ. Barth insists that there is only one covenant, the *covenant of grace* which God established by taking mankind into partnership with Himself in virtue of the union of divine and human nature in Jesus Christ. All God's dealings with men hinge upon this event. It is, therefore, Barth argues, a profound mistake to think of Adam as being in any way autonomous. Indeed, in Barth's hands he shrinks to a pale shadow of his former self. He is no longer a historical, individual figure, but a reflection of every man.

> The Bible gives to this story and to all men in this sense the general title of Adam. Adam is mentioned relatively seldom both in the Old Testament and the New. There are only two passages which treat him explicitly: Genesis 2–3 and Romans 5: 12–21 (to which we might add 1 Corinthians 15: 22 and 43). The meaning of Adam is simply man, and as the bearer of this name which denotes the being and essence of all other men, Adam appears in the Genesis story as the man who owes his existence directly to the creative will and Word and act of God without any human intervention, the man who is to that extent the first man . . . But it is the name of Adam the transgressor which God gives to world-history as a whole. The name Adam sums up this history as the history of mankind which God has given up, given up to its pride on account of its pride.

[1] *Cf.* H. Heppe, *op. cit.*, pp. 371–409 for the views of the seventeenth-century Reformed theologians on this.

It sums up the meaning or meaninglessness of this history
. . . There never was a golden age. There is no point in
looking back to one. The first man was immediately the
first sinner.[2]

There was never, Barth holds, any state of original righteousness.[3] Nor indeed may we regard original sin as a sort
of hereditary disease.[4] All these errors of orthodoxy stem
from the same root: failure to see that there is only one
principle underlying God's dealings with men – Jesus Christ.
In this way Barth meticulously works out the logical
implications of his Christocentric premise. In the next few
pages we shall see how he rigorously applies it to other
aspects of man, creation and reconciliation. But it is worth
while pausing to ask whether this Christocentric scheme of
reality is shared by the biblical writers from whom Barth
claims to have derived his theology. Again the answer must
be in the negative. In the first instance, Barth's case hinges
upon his view of the *covenant* and election. We have already
seen that the biblical writers do not envisage the inclusion
of all mankind in either of these concepts.[5] In the second
place, Barth's treatment of Adam does less than justice to
the biblical data.[6] At whatever point of time we may try

---

[2] *C.D.*, IV, 1, pp. 507f. This basic position is elaborated at length in Barth's
paper *Christ and Adam: Man and Humanity in Romans 5*, Eng. tr. by T. A. Smail
(Oliver and Boyd, 1956) (*S.J.T. Occasional Papers No. 5*).
[3] *C.D.*, IV, 1, pp. 499–513.   [4] *C.D.*, IV, 1, pp. 499ff.
[5] See above, pp. 101–108.
[6] For a critique of Barth's treatment of Adam see John Murray, 'Karl Barth
on Romans 5' in *The Epistle to the Romans: The English Text with Introduction,
Exposition and Notes* (Marshall, Morgan and Scott, 1960), I, Appendix D, pp.
384–390; *cf.* also the article on 'Adam' in *The New Bible Dictionary*, pp. 13f.
by John Murray and T. C. Mitchell. For discussion of this question from the
viewpoint of anthropology see B. Ramm, *The Christian View of Science and
Scripture* (Paternoster, 1955), pp. 214–242; *Modern Science and Christian Faith: A
Symposium on the Relationship of the Bible to Modern Science*, by members of the
American Scientific Affiliation (Van Kampen, Wheaton Illinois, 1950³), pp.
98–195; and the following articles in *Faith and Thought: Journal of the Victoria
Institute*: J. Stafford Wright, 'An Examination for Religious Beliefs of
Palaeolithic Man', Vol. 90, No. 1, Spring 1958, pp. 4–15; T. C. Mitchell,
'Archaeology and Genesis I–XI', Vol. 91, No. 1, Summer 1959, pp. 28–49
and Vol. 91, Nos. 2–3, Winter 1959 – Summer 1960, pp. 125–129; J. M. Clark,
'Genesis and its Underlying Realities', Vol. 93, No. 3, Summer 1964, pp.

to place him, the references to Adam in the Bible point to a definite figure whose actions in some way implicated the rest of humanity. And in the third place, the New Testament does not speak of all men as if they are in Christ already. Man is not in Christ by nature but by spiritual rebirth.[7] By nature a man is a child of wrath; he receives forgiveness and life only as he turns to Christ in faith.

b. Man

Barth's view of man is merely the outworking of what has gone before. In view of the *covenant* and election Barth concludes: 'Man's essential and original nature is to be found, therefore, not in Adam but in Christ.'[8] If, therefore, we want to understand man, we must first look not at man as he is by himself, nor even at isolated pronouncements on him in Scripture, but at man as Barth sees him in Christ. Jesus Christ is the 'prototype' of humanity: [9]

> The nature of the man Jesus is the key to the problem of the human. This man is man. As certainly as God's relation to sinful man is properly and primarily His relation to this man alone, and a relation to the rest of mankind only in Him and through Him, He alone is primarily and properly man.[1]

In other words, the doctrine of man is really an aspect of Christology.[2]

There is no need to dwell on this in detail in view of the scope of this essay. We shall consider an aspect of it when

---

146-158 and Vol. 94, Nos. 1-2, Spring 1965, pp. 135-141. Interpretations of the opening chapters of Genesis along symbolical, though not necessarily absolutely unhistorical lines have been made by conservative scholars in *Is There a Conflict between Genesis I and Natural Science?* by N. H. Ridderbos (Eerdmans, Grand Rapids, 1957), and D. F. Payne, *Genesis One Reconsidered* (Tyndale Press, 1964).

[7] *Cf.* (*e.g.*) Matthew 7:13-27; 25:31-46; John 1:5, 12ff.; 3:3-21; 6:35-58; Acts 2:38ff.; 4:12; Romans 1:16; 6:11; Galatians 2:16ff.; 3:6-14; 4:4ff.; Ephesians 2:1-10; 2 Corinthians 3:15ff.; 4:3ff.; 5:11-21; Hebrews 10:12-39; 1 Peter 2:9ff.; 1 John 1:5; 2:17; 3:14ff.

[8] *Christ and Adam*, p. 6.   [9] *C.D.*, III, 2, p. 50.   [1] *C.D.*, III, 2, p. 43.

[2] *C.D.*, III, 2, p. 44.

we look at Barth's view of law and gospel.[3] It is sufficient to point out that Barth himself follows out this procedure down to the minutest detail. In the volume of the *Church Dogmatics* devoted to man he begins by setting out this general line of approach,[4] and then treats man as a creature.[5] Next he proceeds to retrace his steps over the now familiar ground of the covenant, this time working it out under the heading 'Man in his Determination as the Covenant-Partner of God'.[6] Finally he looks at 'Man as Soul and Body'[7] and 'Man in his Time'.[8] In each of these sections he begins by devoting a sub-section to Jesus in the light of the particular issue and then proceeds to apply what he sees like a paradigm. We may sum up his approach by citing the five summary theses which preface each of these sections on man:

Because man, living under heaven and on earth, is the creature whose relation to God is revealed to us in the Word of God, he is the central object of the theological doctrine of creation. As the man Jesus is Himself the revealing Word of God, He is the source of our knowledge of the nature of man as created by God.[9]

The being of man is the history which shows how one of God's creatures, elected and called by God, is caught up in personal responsibility before Him and proves itself capable of fulfilling it.[1]

That real man is determined by God for life with God has its inviolable correspondence in the fact that his creaturely being is a being in encounter – between I and Thou, man and woman. It is human in this encounter, and in this humanity it is a likeness of the being of its Creator and a being in hope in Him.[2]

Through the Spirit of God, man is the subject, form and life of a substantial organism, the soul of his body – wholly and simultaneously both, in inescapable difference, inseparable unity, and indestructible order.[3]

Man lives in the allotted span of his present, past and future life. He who was before him and will be after him,

---

3 See below, pp. 126–130.
5 *C.D.*, III, 2, pp. 55–202.
7 *C.D.*, III, 2, pp. 325–436.
9 *C.D.*, III, 2, p. 3.
2 *C.D.*, III, 2, p. 203.

4 *C.D.*, III, 2, pp. 3–54.
6 *C.D.*, III, 2, pp. 203–324.
8 *C.D.*, III, 2, pp. 437–640.
1 *C.D.*, III, 2, p. 55.
3 *C.D.*, III, 2, p. 325.

and who therefore fixes the boundaries of his being, is the eternal God, his Creator and Covenant-partner. He is the hope in which man may live in his time.[4]

c. Sin and evil[5]

Whatever judgment posterity may pass on Barth, no critic may deny the originality and resolution which he brings to the task of expounding the whole of reality in relation to its ground and its goal, Jesus Christ. And it is as the reverse side of this Christ-centred reality that Barth intends us to understand the nature of sin and evil which emanate from what Barth calls *chaos*. Or rather, *chaos* is that which lacks reality precisely because God passed it by in the act of creation. At the beginning of all things stands the will of God which brought the universe into being so that man might live in communion with God through Jesus Christ. In virtue of this act the world stands in a positive relationship with God. On the other hand:

Everything else, i.e. everything neutral or hostile to God's purpose, ceased to be when time commenced with this divine volition and accomplishment, and the world was fashioned and ordered by God in time. It is that which, denied by God's will and act, belongs only to the non-recurring past of commencing time. It is that which is excluded from all present and future existence, i.e. chaos, the world fashioned otherwise than according to the divine purpose, and therefore formless and intrinsically impossible. If even the world willed and posited by God as His creation is not itself divine in virtue of its creation, it is at least preserved from the necessity or possibility of being ungodly or anti-godly. That which is ungodly and antigodly can have reality only as that which by God's

---

[4] *C.D.*, III, 2, p. 437.

[5] On the problem of evil see especially *C.D.*, III, 3, pp. 289–368. Barth's main teaching on sin occurs at various points within the context of his teaching on reconciliation (*cf. C.D.*, IV, 1, pp. 358–513; *C.D.*, IV, 2, pp. 378–498; *C.D.*, IV, 3, pp. 368–478). For further discussion see especially Herbert Hartwell, *The Theology of Karl Barth: An Introduction* (Duckworth, 1964), pp. 116–123, 139ff.; G. C. Berkouwer, *The Triumph of Grace in the Theology of Karl Barth*, Eng. tr. by Harry R. Boer (Paternoster, 1956), pp. 79–88, 215–261, 370–383 and *passim*; John Hick, *Evil and the God of Love* (Macmillan, 1966), pp. 132–150.

decision and operation has been rejected and has dis-
appeared, and therefore only as a frontier of that which is
and will be according to God's decision and action.[6]

Chaos possesses a quasi-reality in virtue of the fact that God
rejected it. In this sense it is the proper object of the wrath
of God, since it owes its nature to the divine judgment which
is the reverse side of God's election of creation in Jesus
Christ.[7] Chaos eludes definition precisely because it is nothingness, because it is irrational and absurd, because it has
no real part with God's creation.[8] But in the light of revelation it may be circumscribed by use of such terms as *nothingness (das Nichtige)* and *evil (das Böse)*.[9]

Creation, on the other hand, might be described as a
triumph of grace.[1] For it is in virtue of the covenant of
grace in Jesus Christ that the creation comes into being and
in virtue of this that it is preserved from *nothingness*. Moreover, it is against this background concept of grace that
Barth understands sin. Although explanation is precluded
by its absurd character, sin may be broadly designated as
'the self-surrender of the creature to nothingness',[2] 'the in-
ruption of chaos into the sphere of creation, the establishment of the counter-regime of that which is not, of that
which God has denied and rejected, radical evil, that which
is opposed to God and His work.'[3] Or again: 'Sin is that
which is absurd, man's absurd choice and decision for that
which is not, described in the Genesis story as his hearkening
to the voice of the serpent, the beast of chaos. Sin exists only
in this absurd event.'[4]

Barth also speaks of the 'ontological impossibility' of sin.[5]

---

[6] *C.D.*, III, 1, pp. 101f. Barth here is commenting upon Genesis 1:2.

[7] *C.D.*, III, 3, pp. 351ff.

[8] *C.D.*, III, 3, pp. 302–349; *cf. C.D.*, IV, 3, p. 177.

[9] *C.D.*, III, 3, pp. 289ff. and *passim*. Barth is careful to distinguish his view of *nothingness* from the various concepts of the Nought in philosophy (*cf. ibid.*, pp. 312–348).

[1] G. C. Berkouwer sees the triumph of grace as the leitmotiv of Barth's theology. Accordingly he expounds Barth's doctrine of creation under the heading 'The Triumph of Grace in Creation' (*op. cit.*, pp. 52–88).

[2] *C.D.*, IV, 1, p. 79.   [3] *C.D.*, IV, 1, p. 436; *cf.* p. 411.

[4] *C.D.*, IV, 1, p. 410.   [5] *C.D.*, III, 2, p. 136.

By this he does not mean that there are no such things as sin and evil, even though the term suggests this. Nor is he thinking of the metaphysical problem of reconciling the existence of evil with the idea of an omnipotent, benevolent deity. Revelation in Jesus Christ leaves no room in Barth's thinking for abstract metaphysical speculation. Sin and chaos are rendered 'ontologically impossible' by the prior gracious relationship, established once and for all in view of Jesus Christ. The 'ontological impossibility' of sin is, therefore, grounded in Christology. The godlessness of sin is a pseudo-godlessness. Sin and godlessness do exist, but because of man's being in the covenant, their existence is only relative.[6] Sinful man does indeed strive for release from the covenant, but he cannot escape from his being in grace.[7] Sin is therefore a reaction against grace. It is not a contingency which saving grace is designed to meet but an attempt to evade the very ground of man's being. It is an evasion of grace. It is a denial of that which cannot be denied, a looking past the Word of God to the state of chaos, an involvement with the impossible.[8]

In view of all this, it will be readily appreciated that it is no accident that Barth places his main studies of sin in the context of his doctrine of reconciliation.[9] Not only does its character only really come to light in view of Christ's reconciling work.[1] It is a reaction to the grace of God revealed in that work.[2]

In his exposition of sin Barth seeks to avoid two extremes which, in his opinion, are as opposite as they are erroneous. On the one hand, sin must not be underestimated. In making this point, Barth renounces all affinity with the

---

[6] *Ibid.*; *cf. C.D.*, III, 3, pp. 351ff., 363ff.

[7] *C.D.*, IV, 1, p. 540. Berkouwer aptly sums up Barth's view: 'The most important thing is not God's reaction to sin, but His *faithfulness* which sin, as a "coming between", *is not able to annul*' (*op. cit.*, p. 248; *cf. C.D.*, IV, 1, pp. 22–78).

[8] *C.D.*, IV, 1, pp. 514–642; note especially, pp. 540ff.

[9] See above, pp. 26f., 119, n. 5.

[1] *Cf. C.D.*, IV, 1, pp. 358–413; *C.D.*, IV, 2, pp. 378–403; *C.D.*, IV, 3, pp. 368–434.

[2] *Cf. C.D.*, IV, 1, pp. 414ff.; *C.D.*, IV, 2, pp. 403ff.; *C.D.*, IV, 3, pp. 434ff.

optimistic liberalism which regarded sin and evil as a kind of mental aberration or growing pain in the evolution of religion.[3] Chaos is the object of the wrath of God. The gravity of sin can only be appreciated in the light of the cross. But for that reason the importance of sin must not be overestimated. The cross reveals the impotence of sin and the destruction of chaos.[4] Sin may involve a fall, but not a falling away.[5] Such an eventuality is precluded by the covenant.[6] The goodness and existence of the creation are secured in Jesus Christ as creator, creature and reconciler. Therefore, there can be no room for anxiety in the Christian. What Barth writes with regard to world affairs is typical of his whole outlook on life: so far as the present-day conflict is concerned between Russia and America, a single hymn by Paul Gerhardt is stronger than the worst thing we have read or ever will read in the papers or experience for ourselves.[7]

This joyful confidence in Christ, come what may, re-echoes that of Paul when he wrote that nothing can separate us from the love of God in Christ Jesus our Lord,[8] and that care of the Father which Jesus commended to His disciples, urging them not to be anxious.[9] But it must be asked whether this confidence is grounded in the same thing. In a broad sense the answer is Yes, in so far at it springs from the love of God in Christ which has and will overcome every evil. But in the narrower sense – in the sense of inquiring into the route which Barth took to arrive at this conclusion – the answer is somewhat dubious.

For although Barth claims that evil is inexplicable he goes a good deal further than either Jesus or Paul or any other biblical writer to explain it.[1] The latter make no attempt to explain the existence of evil. Like the reason for the existence of God it is beyond human comprehension.

---

[3] *C.D.*, II, 1, pp. 363ff.; *cf.* Berkouwer, *op. cit.*, pp. 235ff.
[4] *C.D.*, IV, 1, pp. 83f.   [5] *C.D.*, IV, 1, pp. 481ff.   [6] *C.D.*, III, 2, p. 136.
[7] *Die Kirche zwischen Ost und West* (Evangelischer Verlag, Zollikon-Zürich, 1949), pp. 8f.
[8] Romans 8:38f.; *cf.* Philippians 1:21; 4:11–13.
[9] Matthew 6:25ff.; 10:22f.; Luke 12:6f. *etc.*
[1] *Cf.* G. C. Berkouwer, *op. cit.*, pp. 221ff., 244ff.

The biblical writers are confident that God will finally over-throw the evil powers in view of the finished work of Christ.[2] But they do not begin to explain how evil came into being. Similarly, sin is depicted as transgression, disobedience and even debt which brings alienation from God and puts man into bondage to evil.[3] But the biblical writers never attempt to explain the ultimate origin of sin and evil. They are there as man's enemies. We know something of what they involve. But ultimately they are mysteries. By contrast, Barth undertakes to explain them and fit them into his scheme of reality. They are, in a fact, a corollary of his concepts of crea-tion and covenant. The term *nothingness* is symptomatic of the whole undertaking. Symptomatic too is Barth's view of evil beings. Demons are not fallen beings which have a real created existence, but only the quasi-existence which per-tains to *nothingness*.[4] But as all this is put forward as a piece of biblical theology, the question must be asked whether it would still stand if Barth's view of creation and covenant were to prove untenable. The present writer, at least, doubts it very much. It would seem that the old view of the coven-ant of works[5] with its corollary of sin as transgression and grace as the divine answer to man's need comes much closer to the biblical perspective.

III THE INCARNATION, THE COVENANT
AND RECONCILIATION

The final main topic in our survey of Barth's teaching which calls for consideration is his doctrine of reconciliation. There is much here which deserves special attention, such as his view of the offices of Christ[6] and his states of humiliation

---

[2] *Cf.* Luke 10:18; Romans 16:20; 1 Corinthians 15:24–28; Colossians 2:14ff.; Revelation 19:20; 20:14.

[3] Genesis 3; Matthew 6:12; John 8:34, 36; Romans 1:18ff.; 4:15; 5:14–21; 6:12–23; Galatians 2:16ff.; Ephesians 2:1–3; Colossians 2:14f.; Hebrews 2:2; 1 John 3:4.

[4] Whereas angels are real creatures and have a positive being, the demons do not (*C.D.*, III, 3, pp. 369–531). Despite Jude 6 and 2 Peter 2:4, Barth claims that 'The demons merely act as if they came from heaven' (*ibid.*, p. 531). But see also Berkouwer, *op. cit.*, 76–80.

[5] See above, pp. 113–117.

[6] *Cf.* above, pp. 26f.

and exaltation[7] in which Barth looks first at Christ and then at man as his life is bound up with his being in Christ. But comment must be restricted. And perhaps we shall see best the main thrust of Barth's thought if we confine ourselves to the three phases of reconciliation: its origin in the purposes of God and the work of Christ, the outworking of reconciliation in the present, and the final outcome of reconciliation. We shall do this under these three headings: *a. Double predestination and the cross; b. Gospel and law; c. Universalism?* The precise significance of these terms will emerge as we explore Barth's message.

a. Double predestination and the cross

We have already seen how Barth takes over from Reformed theology the ideas of covenant and election and applies them in a radically different way in the light of his understanding of the incarnation.[8] In view of the election of Jesus Christ all mankind is elect, because of the union of divine and human nature in Him. Barth pushes this idea even further by taking up the idea of double predestination. But whereas for Calvin this had meant the election of some men to eternal

---

[7] Barth's whole perspective might be said to be worked out in terms of these states, and therefore his view emerges fully only as the successive part-volumes on Reconciliation are read. But for brief statements see *C.D.*, IV, 1, pp. 133f.; IV, 2, pp. 21, 110. Under the heading, 'Jesus Christ, the Lord as Servant' (*C.D.*, IV, 1, pp. 157–779) Barth looks first at the obedience of the Son of God, His humiliation and death as the judge judged in our place. He then turns to the sin of which this act of the Son of God is the exact opposite – man's pride. Finally he turns to the benefits which Christ's work as Servant brings to man: man's justification and its outworking in the church and in faith through the Holy Spirit. The same symmetrical pattern is followed in the other two sections. Under the heading 'Jesus Christ, the Servant as Lord' (*C.D.*, IV, 2) Barth looks first at the exaltation of the Son of Man. He then turns to the misery and sloth of man which is the opposite of Christ's exalted life. And then he turns to the benefits which this aspect of Christ's work brings: man's sanctification, the Holy Spirit and the upbuilding of the Christian community and the Holy Spirit and love. Under the heading 'Jesus Christ, the True Witness' (*C.D.*, IV, 3) Barth first looks at the glory of the mediator and then by contrast at the falsehood and condemnation of man. He then finally turns again to the benefits which this aspect of Christ brings to man: his vocation, the Holy Spirit and the sending of the Christian community, and the Holy Spirit and Christian hope.

[8] See above, pp. 101–108.

life and the rejection of others, Barth re-interprets it in the light of his basic premise that all God's dealings with men are effected in and through the person of Jesus Christ. For Barth Christ is both elect and reprobate. He is elect for all and reprobate for all. Predestination for Barth means 'the non-rejection of man'.[9]

If the teachers of predestination were right when they spoke always of a duality, of election and reprobation, of predestination to salvation or perdition, to life or death, then we may say already that in the election of Jesus Christ which is the eternal will of God, God has ascribed to man the former, election, salvation and life; and to Himself He has ascribed the latter, reprobation, perdition and death. If it is indeed the case that the divine good-pleasure which was the beginning of all things with God carries with it the risk and threat of negation, then it is so because the Son of God incarnate represents and Himself is this divine good-pleasure. The risk and threat is the portion which the Son of God, i.e. God Himself, has chosen for His own.[1]

This leads on to a substitutionary doctrine of atonement which seeks to do justice both to the holiness and wrath of God and to the all-inclusiveness of Christ's humanity:

The rejection which all men incurred, the wrath of God under which all men lie, the death which all men must die, God in His love for men transfers from all eternity to Him in whom He loves and elects them, and whom He elects at their head and in their place. God from all eternity ordains this obedient One in order that He might bear the suffering which the disobedient have deserved and which for the sake of God's righteousness must necessarily be borne. Indeed, the very obedience which was exacted of Him and attained by Him was His willingness to take upon Himself the divine rejection of all others and to suffer that which they ought to have suffered.[2]

[9] C.D., II, 2, p. 167.   [1] C.D., II, 2, p. 162f.
[2] C.D., II, 2, p. 123; cf. C.D., IV, 1, pp. 211–283 on 'The Judge Judged in our Place'.

There can be no doubt that Barth has deep insight into the significance of the cross. We shall, however, postpone considering the implications of his teaching until we come to consider its universalistic implications. Before doing this, we shall consider the way this affects the preaching of the gospel and law in the present.

b. Gospel and law

We now turn to another aspect of reconciliation, Barth's understanding of gospel and law. Here we look at the way reconciliation comes to man in the present. And here again Barth's view turns upside down the approach he inherited from his Reformed forefathers.

Protestant theology has long been accustomed to thinking of the Christian message in terms of law and gospel. The approach goes back to the Reformers themselves who in turn had no difficulty in showing that this approach was one used by the biblical writers themselves.[3] The law comes first to man to prepare the way for Christ. It shows him as he really is in the light of God's holy character. It convicts of guilt as a necessary first step to make a man ready for the message of grace.[4]

Karl Barth reverses this. Instead of speaking of *law and gospel*, he inverts the order and speaks of *gospel and law*. Warning of this new procedure came as early as 1935 with the publication of the paper *Evangelium und Gesetz*.[5] Barth's programme is simple. It is entirely in line with what we have seen of his later developments. It consists of bringing the church's understanding of law and gospel into harmony with the way Jesus Christ is understood as both

---

[3] *Cf.* Luther, *A Commentary on St. Paul's Epistle to the Galatians*, Eng. tr. edited by Philip S. Watson (James Clarke, 1953), pp. 324ff.; Calvin, *Institutes of the Christian Religion*, II, vii; see further Philip S. Watson, *Let God be God: An Interpretation of the Theology of Martin Luther* (Epworth, 1947), pp. 152–160; and for criticism of Barth in this respect Gustaf Wingren, *Theology in Conflict; Nygren, Barth, Bultmann*, Eng. tr. by E. H. Wahlstrom (Oliver and Boyd, 1958), pp. 33ff., 110–128.

[4] *Cf.* (*e.g.*) John 1:17; Romans 2:1–6:23; 10:4; 1 Corinthians 15:56f.; Galatians 2:11–4:31.

[5] 'Gospel and Law' in *God, Grace and Gospel*, translated by J. S. McNab (Oliver and Boyd, 1959) (*S.J.T. Occasional Papers No. 8*), pp. 3–27.

revelation and reconciliation. Barth begins with a reminder
that in point of time the Mosaic law was preceded by the
promise of grace made to Abraham.[6] But in fact this was
already undergirded by God's *covenant* relationship with
man in Jesus Christ.[7] In view of the retrospective and pros-
pective significance of Jesus Christ, it can never be said that
there was a time when the Word of God did not come to
man as a word of grace, calling upon man to realize the
gracious relationship in which he stands in Jesus Christ. In
his exposition of this relationship the crucial factor for
Barth is Christ's fulfilment of the law:

> We have to start with the indubitable witness of Scripture
> that Jesus Christ (of whom we have heard that He is grace,
> that He is the content of the gospel) has satisfied the law,
> has fulfilled the law, which means that He has kept it by
> obeying its commandments. When we are concerned with
> defining the law, we must in no case minimize the fact
> that Jesus Christ, while He was 'the manifested grace of
> God' (Titus 2 : 11), kept at the same time the command-
> ments of the law. Rather we shall have to start out from
> this fact. It will not only form the criterion for measuring
> all conceptions that we ourselves have fashioned of law
> and standards of conduct. It will have to be the canon for
> the interpretation of all that meets us as law in the Old
> Testament and the New.[8]

Furthermore, it becomes clear as the exposition proceeds
that in virtue of Jesus Christ's position as the divinely
elected representative of mankind, Barth regards this fulfilment as universally vicarious. Hence the law may on no
account be regarded as an abstract demand to conform to a
hypothetical norm. Law and gospel are simply different
terms denoting different ways of looking at Jesus Christ.
Whereas gospel refers to the fact that the will of God is
universally realized in the person of Jesus Christ, the term
law denotes an implication of this fact.

> When we see here, i.e. in the life of Christ, the will of
> God being done, when, that is, we see His grace in action,

[6] *Op. cit.*, p. 3.   [7] *Op. cit.*, pp. 4ff.   [8] *Op. cit.*, p. 8.

the law is manifested to us. From what God here does for us, we learn what God wants with us and of us . . . His action does not revolve within Himself, but is aimed at *our* action, at getting our action into conformity with Him. 'Be ye – more accurately, *ye shall be* – perfect, as your heavenly Father is perfect' (Matthew 5:48). It is impossible for grace to become known to men without carrying with it this impetus, without exciting to this future: ye shall be! Indeed, the very revelation of grace is this impetus. If the indicative holds good, 'that I am not my own but belong to my true Saviour Jesus Christ', then its validity establishes the imperative – the Ten Commandments, as also the interpretation of them in the Sermon on the Mount and the application of them in the instructions given by the Apostles.[9]

This line of thought has prompted Barth to coin two sets of concepts to express the general relationship of gospel and law. The first set, *imperative* and *indicative*, is exemplified in the above quotation. The second set is the somewhat ambiguous antithesis, *form* and *content*:

The Law is nothing else than the necessary form of the Gospel, whose content is grace. It is just this content that enforces this form, the form which calls for a like form, the form of law.[1]

Whatever may be the merits or demerits of Barth's terminology, it is clear that Barth's revision of the traditional language involves more than a change of vocabulary. The law is a summons to participate in the gospel. But it is not the sort of summons that is usually accorded to the law in Protestant orthodoxy, viz to convict of sin as a prior preparation for the gospel. Any similar function the law may perform is in fact a by-product of its real work. Its true function is to call men to realize their true being which they have already in Jesus Christ.

9 *Op. cit.*, pp. 8f.
1 *Op. cit.*, p. 10; *cf. C.D.*, II, 2, p. 511. In his essay, '*Zur Einheit von Gesetz und Evangelium*', in *Antwort*, pp. 287–309, H. Gollwitzer complains that this contrast could import the false antithesis of essential and non-essential into the argument which is not part of Barth's intention.

This, in fact, is the essence of Barth's concept of ethics:

It is the Christian doctrine of God, or, more exactly, the knowledge of the electing grace of God in Jesus Christ, which decides the nature and aim of theological ethics, of ethics as an element of Church dogmatics. It has its basis, therefore, in the doctrine of God Himself. For the God who claims man makes Himself originally responsible for man. The fact that He gives man His command, that He subjects man to His command, means that He makes Himself responsible not only for its authority but also for its fulfilment. . . . Now the matter of theological ethics is the responsibility which God has assumed for us in the fact that He has made us accountable through His command. Its matter is the Word and work of God in Jesus Christ, in which the right action of man has already been performed and therefore waits only to be confirmed by our action.[2]

The significance of this last point is brought out a few pages earlier on in the same volume of the *Church Dogmatics.* Jesus Christ

is the electing God and elected man in One. But He is also the sanctifying God and the sanctified man in One . . . The grace of Jesus Christ itself and alone is the reality in which from the very start man himself has his reality. The man to whom the Word of God is directed and for whom the work of God was done – it is all one whether we are thinking of the Christian who has grasped it in faith and related it to himself, or the man in the cosmos who has not yet done so – this man, in virtue of this Word and work, does not exist by himself. He is not an independent subject, to be considered independently. In virtue of the death and resurrection of Jesus Christ – whether he knows it and believes it or not – it is simply not true that he belongs to himself and is left to himself, that he is thrown back on himself. He belongs to the Head, Jesus Christ, of whose body he is or is to become a member, the Lord of the Church who is also the Lord of the cosmos, and therefore the Lord of those who so far do not believe in Him, or do so no longer. He exists because

[2] *C.D.*, II, 2, p. 543; *cf. op. cit.*, pp. 9, 14.

> Jesus Christ exists. He exists as a predicate of this Subject,
> i.e. that which has been decided and is real for man in
> this Subject is true for him. Therefore the divine com-
> mand as it is directed to him, as it applies to him consists
> in his relationship to this Subject . . . The ethical problem
> of Church dogmatics can consist only in the question
> whether and to what extent human action is a glorifica-
> tion of the grace of Jesus Christ.[3]

This conception of ethics as the realization of man's true
nature which he has already in Christ is worked out in
detail in the various sections of the *Church Dogmatics*
which are devoted to ethics.[4] Conversely, Barth rejects all
conceptions of general ethics which try to work out notions
of good and of right conduct apart from man's existence in
grace. In point of fact, such attempts to work out ways of life
coincide exactly with Barth's idea of sin.[5] For they mean
that man was trying to live as if he were not the object of
grace. They are the denial of grace.

Thus Barth's ethics is a further extension of the principle
that all God's dealings with men are effected in and through
the person of Christ. It is not merely a matter of revelation,
in the sense that the gospel reveals a higher code of
behaviour than any other known to man. It is not that the
Bible imparts certain otherwise unknown principles and
items of information. It is a question of man living out his
true nature in Christ. Man can only do this by grounding
his ethics upon the gospel. But fundamentally the noetic is
grounded in the ontic. The knowledge of what man is to be
is based, according to Barth, on what man already is and
has had done for him in Christ.

c. Universalism?

All that we have said so far about the election of man to be
God's covenant partner, the double predestination of Christ
to be both elect for all and reprobate for all, and of ethics
being the confirmation, the realization of man's existence in

---

[3] *C.D.*, II, 2, pp. 538ff.
[4] *C.D.*, II, 2, pp. 509–781; *C.D.*, III, 4; see also Barth's treatment of Christian
conduct in each of the part-volumes of *C.D.*, IV on reconciliation.
[5] *C.D.*, II, 2, p. 518; and see generally pp. 509–542.

grace would seem to suggest that Barth believes in the universal salvation of all men through Christ. This impression is not weakened by the way Barth talks about the righteousness of God and justification. He defines the former as

the final righteous decision of God, which, for everyone who acknowledges it in faith, is the power of God unto salvation.[6]

Accordingly, justification by faith is construed as

conforming to the decision about them that has already been made in Him.[7]
In sovereign anticipation of our faith God has justified us through the sacrificial blood of Christ.[8]

In other words, it is a matter of man conforming in time to a *decision* which has been taken by God in eternity. Those who conform enjoy the benefits of what God offers, but those who do not are not necessarily precluded for ever. In line with this is Barth's description of the incarnation (with its implied union of God and man) as God's *decision* about man.[9] Similarly, the resurrection of Christ is God's *verdict* on man in view of Christ's death in his place.[1]

The main thrust of Barth's thinking is caught in a statement like this:

We are no longer free, then, to think of God's eternal election as bifurcating into a rightward and a leftward election. There is a leftward election. But God willed that the object of this election should be Himself and not man. God removed from man and took upon Himself the burden of the evil which unavoidably threatened and actually achieved and exercised dominion in the world that He had ordained as the theatre of His glory. God removed from man and took upon Himself the suffering which resulted from this dominion, including the condemnation of sinful man. For this reason we cannot ascribe any

[6] *Christ and Adam*, p. 1.   [7] *Op. cit.*, p. 3.   [8] *Op. cit.*, p. 2.
[9] *C.D.*, II, 2, p. 7.   [1] *C.D.*, IV, 1, p. 309.

autonomy to the world of evil, or to the will of God as
it is directed towards and assents to it in a permissive
form. In Jesus Christ we can see and know this whole
sphere of evil as something which has already been overcome, something which yields, something which has been
destroyed by the positive will of God's overflowing glory.
And what it is in Jesus Christ it is also in the beginning
with God. And for this reason in God's decree at the
beginning there is for man only a predestination which
corresponds to the perfect being of God Himself; a predestination to His kingdom and to blessedness and life.
Any other predestination is merely presumed and unreal;
a predestination arising from sin and error and opposed
by the revelation of God; not the divine predestination
fulfilled in God's eternal decree. Man takes upon him
something which God has reserved for Himself if he tries
to enter into this predestination or to think himself as
predestined to sin and death.[2]

If this line of thought brings Barth to the brink of universalism, he hesitates to take the final step. On the one hand,
he takes in an all-inclusive sense such biblical passages as
Colossians 1 : 19f.;[3] John 1 : 9, 29; 3 : 16f.; 4 : 42; 6 : 33;
8 : 12; 9 : 5; 11 : 9; 12 : 46; 2 Corinthians 5 : 19; 1 Timothy
2 : 4; and 1 John 2 : 2.[4] But on the other hand, Barth shrinks
from compromising the sovereign freedom of God by committing himself either to the universal salvation of all mankind or to limited atonement for an elect number.[5] Hence a
certain air of ambiguity surrounds his teaching. Although
Barth's detailed study of the last things has yet to appear,
it would seem that his way of resolving the difficulty lies
along the line of the hint contained in the last sentence of
the above extract. Man as such can never be rejected. Man
as such can never know the wrath and desolation which
Christ knew on the cross. For Christ has taken it all upon
Himself. Hence, if there are individuals who go on rejecting
the free forgiveness offered them in Christ, they are doing
the impossible. They are trying to live the life of the rejected even though they are not. This train of thought is

---

[2] *C.D.*, II, 2, pp. 172f.   [3] *God, Grace and Gospel*, p. 49.
[4] *C.D.*, II, 2, pp. 421f.   [5] *C.D.*, II, 2, pp. 417, 422.

sketched out in a section on 'The Elect and the Rejected'.[6]
It is summed up in the following words:

> Rejected individuals as such (those who live the life of
> the rejected) are the evidence of the sin for which He has
> made Himself responsible, of the punishment which He
> has borne. In the last resort, in so far as it seems to indicate
> their own perdition and abandonment by God, their wit-
> ness can only be false. For to be genuinely and actually
> abandoned by God, cannot be their concern, since it is
> the concern of Jesus Christ. Therefore even this false
> witness cannot help pointing to Jesus Christ as the One
> who properly and actually was the lost and abandoned
> sinner, whose shadow lies upon them. Thus for all their
> godlessness, they are unable to restore the perversity for
> whose removal He surrendered Himself, and so rekindle
> the fire of divine wrath which He has borne in this self-
> sacrifice. In their sinning, and in their suffering as sinners,
> they can only be arrogant and yet reluctant participants
> in the rejection which He has averted from them by taking
> it upon Himself in the consummation of His election.
> They cannot help the fact that objectively and actually
> they are themselves witnesses to His election. It is not
> without Him that they, too, are what they are. It is only
> figuratively and secondarily that they can be what He
> alone is primarily and properly. He is *the* Rejected, as and
> because He is *the* Elect. In view of His election, there is
> no other rejected but Himself.[7]

Given Barth's premises, the logic of this position cannot
be gainsaid. Even apart from Barth's view of the covenant,
this doctrine would appear to be the logical conclusion of
the traditional Arminian interpretation of the atonement
that on the cross Christ died for all men. If He died for all
men in this way, then the wrath of God that Christ knew
will never be known again. But the question must be asked
whether this is the Christian message to the world today
and whether it is the message to which the New Testament
bears witness. This, after all, is the criterion by which Barth
himself insists that all theology must be judged. We shall
therefore conclude this study with a brief assessment of
Barth's position in the light of the New Testament.

[6] *C.D.*, II, 2, pp. 340–409.   [7] *C.D.*, II, 2, pp. 352f.

IV ASSESSMENT

Barth's teaching can be looked at from its opposite ends. We may look at it from the beginning, *i.e.*, we can try to fathom the basic ideas from which it originates. Or we may look at the end-product, *i.e.*, the goal to which his views lead. We have already attempted to do the former in passing when we discussed Barth's ideas of the incarnation, the covenant, election and God.[8] We shall now attempt the latter by asking whether these ideas lead to the same point that the New Testament reaches in its teaching on reconciliation.

In the first place, the New Testament does not speak of judgment in the same way that Barth speaks. In virtue of his idea of the covenant Christ bears judgment for all, according to Barth. This seems to be yet another aspect of the outworking of Barth's underlying thought that all God's dealings with men are effected in and through Jesus Christ through whom God's free grace triumphs over all. Judgment is thus re-interpreted in this Christocentric way. But the New Testament speaks of a judgment over and above that which Christ received in His own person. This is not just the awful scrutiny of the lives of believers.[9] It is the judgment of all who are not in Christ and who have rejected God.[1] Jesus and the New Testament writers speak of this judgment in the most solemn way. It affects eternity. It is not merely a matter of man trying to live as if he were not in a state of grace. It would seem to be a graceless existence in the strictest sense of the term. What Barth seems to have done is to misconstrue the universal significance of Christ. Barth has made Him the universal object of judgment. The New Testament depicts Him as the universal criterion of judgment. He is not all things to all men, even though all men have dealings with Him. To all He is judge. But only to those who receive Him, who are in Christ, is He judged in their place.[2]

---

[8] See above, pp. 101–108.

[9] Matthew 16:27; Romans 14:10ff.; 1 Corinthians 3:10–15; 2 Corinthians 5:10.

[1] Matthew 7:13–27; 16:27; 18:4ff.; 25:1–46; Luke 9:62; 10:20; 17:1ff.; John 3:16ff.; 6:39ff.; 12:48; Acts 17:31; Romans 2:1–10; 6:23; 9:1–11:36; Ephesians 2:1–10 (note verse 3); 2 Thessalonians 1:5–12; Hebrews 6:2; 9:27; 10:26–31; 1 Peter 4:5; Jude 4, 6, 21; Revelation 6:17; 20:11–15. See further, Leon Morris, *The Biblical Doctrine of Judgment* (Tyndale Press, 1960).

[2] An important strand of biblical thought depicts Christ as judge (Matthew

In the second place, it may be observed that Barth treats justification in a similar way. We have already said that Barth has deep insight into the mysteries of God's holiness and love as they meet upon the cross.[3] Unlike some modern theologians, Barth does not shirk his obligation as a Christian scholar to take the New Testament seriously at this point. Barth sees the satisfaction of God's holiness by God's own self-giving on the cross as the event upon which man's whole salvation turns.[4] Forgiveness of sin depends upon the death of Christ. But Barth's view of the *covenant* causes him to make a fundamental shift of emphasis. In the New Testament the death of Christ does not automatically confer forgiveness of sin and justification upon mankind. These are attained only by those who respond to the gospel by appropriating them by faith.[5] Barth, on the other hand, treats the

---

25:31–46; John 5:27; Acts 10:42; 17:30f.; Philippians 2:10; 2 Timothy 4:1). But this office is not subsumed under the rejection which Christ took upon Himself or His regal office in reigning in His kingdom (*cf.* Luke 20:17f.; 1 Peter 2:6–8; Matthew 21:42f.; Mark 12:10f.; Acts 4:11; Psalm 118:22f.; John 3:17ff.; 1 Corinthians 15:25ff.; Philippians 2:10f. with the above-mentioned passages).

[3] See above, pp. 125f.

[4] Matthew 26:28; Mark 10:45; John 1:29; 3:16ff.; 6:25–58; Romans 3:25f.; 8:3; 1 Corinthians 15:3; 2 Corinthians 5:18–21; Galatians 1:4; 3:13; Ephesians 1:7; Colossians 1:20; 2:13ff.; Hebrews 2:14ff.; 5:1–10; 9:24–28; 10:19ff.; 1 Peter 1:19; 1 John 2:2; 4:10; Revelation 1:5; 5:9; 7:14. See further James Denney, *The Death of Christ*, revised edition by R. V. G. Tasker (Tyndale Press, 1951); Leon Morris, *The Apostolic Preaching of the Cross* (Tyndale Press, 1955, 1965[3]); *The Cross in the New Testament* (Paternoster, 1965).

[5] Matthew 11:27ff.; John 3:16–21, 36; 5:24, 40; 10:13ff.; Acts 2: 38; 16:30f.; Romans 1:16f.; 3:25; 4:3; 5:11; 8:1ff.; 9:30ff.; 2 Corinthians 5:17–21; Galatians 2:6; 3:6; Ephesians 2:1–10; Hebrews 4:3ff.; 1 Peter 2:10; 4:17f.; 1 John 1:9. It may also be pointed out that even those passages which speak of the all-embracing love of God are qualified in context. Thus the saving love of the world in the first half of John 3:16 is experienced concretely only by those who respond in faith, as the second half of the verse points out. Even a verse like 2 Peter 3:9 need imply no more than that God has no pleasure in the rejection of the wicked. In any case the *all* in this verse might well refer simply to all the readers whom the writer addresses as *you*. The word *all* in the New Testament does duty for a range of meanings which embrace *all* in an absolute sense and *all kinds of* (*cf.* Luke 11:42). In context the point of 1 Timothy 2:4 is God's purpose to save all kinds of men, though not evidently all absolutely.

work of Christ as the objective justification of humanity in general. The decisive factor of human response is taken out of time. Man's response becomes more a matter of whether he has woken up to the fact that he already is forgiven and not as in the New Testament a fundamental transition from a state of enmity with God to reconciliation.

John Murray has pointed out how Barth's view of justification differs significantly from the Pauline view. Commenting on Barth's study, *Christ and Adam*, he writes:

> According to Paul we are justified by faith, and to apply the terms for justification without discrimination to anything else than to that which is correlative with faith and therefore coincident with it is to deviate radically from the sustained emphasis of the apostle. It is true that there is the once-for-all accomplishment in the blood of Christ which is antecedent to faith. Paul calls it the propitiation, the reconciliation, and redemption. But the all but uniform, if not uniform, use of the term 'justification' and its equivalent is to designate that judgment of God of which faith is the instrument. This act of faith is not directed to the fact that we have been justified but is directed to Christ in order that we may be justified (*cf.* Galatians 2 : 16). It is not to be assumed that in the epistle to the Romans the terms δικαιοσύνη, δικαίωσις, δικαίωμα are used synonymously, as Barth apparently assumes (*cf.* p. 20). In 5 : 16 δικαίωμα and in 5 : 18 δικαίωσις refer to God's justifying act. But exegesis neither requires nor allows identification of this act with the δικαιοσύνη θεοῦ of 1 : 17; 3 : 21, 22; 10 : 3. The latter is the justifying righteousness but is to be distinguished from the justifying act.[6]

In other words, history has become with Barth the projection or actualization of the significance of Jesus Christ. Symptomatic of this process is the way in which Barth speaks of Christ as God's *decision, verdict* and *attitude* towards man.[7] What Barth has done is to transpose the action of justification from the encounter of the individual with

---

[6] John Murray, *op. cit.*, p. 385. The passage reference refers to the American edition. In the British edition it is p. 1.

[7] See above, p. 131.

Christ in history to the realm of a super-history where it is objectified, universalized and all but emptied of subjective response.[8] But in so doing, Barth has drastically changed the New Testament message. His approach has the apparent advantage of being able to take much more seriously than the older liberalism the biblical teaching on the wrath of God and the atonement, and at the same time combining it with a form of universalism highly palatable to modern man. The big difficulty is that this is not the message of the New Testament. If what we have said about the New Testament is right, then Barth's gospel can only foster a false and dangerous optimism. It does less than justice to the gospel. It does a great disservice to the outsider by encouraging him to think that his position before God is radically different from what it is. And it does not help the church to see its vocation and message in its true perspective.

These last points lead to our third and final comment. It concerns whether Barth is right in saying that the unbeliever is not under the law but only under the gospel (and to that extent under the law as the *form* of the gospel).[9] The key to Barth's understanding of gospel and law is the thought that the law comes to man as a law that has already been fulfilled by Christ and which, therefore, only requires confirmation by our action. But again Barth can carry this programme through only at the expense of a radical transformation of the New Testament picture. In view of what we have seen already of the latter's view of judgment and justification, man simply as man is not in a condition of saving grace. Even the believer is not in such a state prior to his coming to Christ. The decisive transition from a state of alienation and wrath to one of reconciliation and peace

[8] In making this point, it has not been forgotten that Barth gives lengthy discussions of *faith* (*cf. C.D.*, IV, 1, pp. 740–779). But for Barth the essential difference between the believer and the unbeliever is that the former knows that he has been reconciled, whereas the latter does not and tries to live as if he is not. Of the believer Barth writes: 'Above all, in the midst of other men he is the one who knows the decisive fact – who knows it in this active knowledge of himself – that Jesus Christ died and rose again not only for himself but for them, that it is the world which God has reconciled to Himself in Him' (*C.D.*, IV, 1, p. 779; *cf.* pp. 568–642).

[9] See above, pp. 126ff.

occurs at conversion and incorporation into Christ. Up to that point man was under the law and a stranger to Christ and the gospel. It is only as he becomes united with Christ and thus shares in Christ's death that he is freed from the condemnation of the law.[1] The same objection can be put another way. The New Testament makes it plain that Christ fulfilled the law.[2] It does not say that Christ fulfilled the law for all men.

In making these various points, what we are saying amounts to this, that when we apply certain acid tests to the outworking of Barth's Christocentric, covenant theology, it does not agree with the New Testament. To change the metaphor, Barth's Christocentric theology is like a Procrustean bed. In order to make the New Testament fit upon it, some important doctrines have to be stretched, whilst others have to be lopped off. Ironically, the root of the trouble is the fact that it is Christ-centred. Or rather, the trouble is that all Barth's theology is made to centre around an *idea* of Christ. But it is not exactly the biblical idea of Christ. Instead of reading his theology from the writings of the New Testament, Barth interprets them in the light of a single preconceived principle, the idea that all God's dealings with men are effected in and through the person of Jesus Christ. But even this idea is understood in a particular way. The very centre of Barth's thought is his idea of the *covenant* by which he means a union of God with mankind in view of the union with divine and human nature in the person of Jesus Christ. And because God is sovereign, loving and gracious, this love and grace is projected upon mankind in view of man's being in Christ. All Barth's later theology is really a series of variations on this theme. And in fact, all the queries and objections to Barth's theology in this essay are also really a series of variations on this theme.

As we have seen Barth unfold this key idea, we have questioned both its foundations and its implications. All along the line Barth has attempted to reinterpret Christian

---

[1] Romans 3:19ff.; 6:3ff.; 7:1–6; 8:3f.; 10:4; Galatians 3:10ff., 19 – 4:7; 5:18; Ephesians 2:1–22; Colossians 2:13f.
[2] Matthew 5:17f.; Romans 15:8; Galatians 3:13 and the passages noted above in n. 1.

theology in accordance with this *single* Christ-principle. But as we have looked at Barth's key ideas we have been led to question whether God does work on the basis of a single principle. Whilst God deals with men through Christ, Christ is not equally all things to all men. To some He is Saviour, to others He is Judge. According to the witness of the New Testament writers, God deals with men in two ways. He deals with them as they are in themselves apart from Christ. And he deals with them as they are in Christ. The two spheres are not identical. They overlap. All men are by nature in the first. Some are by grace in the second.

In making this point, we are saying nothing at all that is new. This is the common theme of traditional evangelical and catholic teaching. It is firmly rooted in Scripture. The basic difference between Karl Barth and traditional Protestant theology lies, therefore, not only in his doctrine of the Word of God. Barth has, in fact, more in common with traditional Protestantism on this score than is sometimes imagined. Whilst there are vital differences, there are things that evangelical theology could learn from Barth without any surrender of vital principle. The basic difference lies in Barth's understanding of the significance of Christ. It is summed up in the contrast between the older idea of the two covenants – the covenant of works and the covenant of grace –and Barth's idea of the single, all-embracing covenant of grace in Christ.[3] However much this older idea might need restatement in modern terms, this is the focal point of conflict between orthodoxy and Barthianism. (It is probably also the unconscious point of conflict between evangelicalism and a good deal of modern theology.) But if the analysis of this essay is correct, the way forward to a deeper understanding of the Christian message in the modern world lies not with Barth's teaching as it stands but with the doctrines which Barth has brought again to the forefront. It lies with the need for a deeper understanding of the covenant theology of the Bible. For in the last analysis, Barth is guilty of Brunner's charge (a charge which Brunner is himself open to) that he has erected a 'Natural Theology on the basis of a statement which has a Biblical core'.[4]

[3] See above, pp. 101ff., 113–117.   [4] *The Christian Doctrine of God*, p. 351.

What is the significance of Karl Barth? As a writer he can be dazzlingly brilliant. He can also be cumbersome and long-winded. One has only to look at some of the excerpts quoted in this study to get the point. Even Barth's most fervent admirers will admit that out of his five hundred and more published writings half, perhaps three-quarters, have already dropped into oblivion. To some theologians Barth's *Church Dogmatics* are a gigantic white elephant. They give up even before they start it not because of its teaching but because of its enormous bulk. The loss is theirs. But even so, the work might have gained twice as much had it been half the size. To my mind, the brief, small-print passages where Barth comments on aspects of Scripture and the views of philosophers and theologians down the ages are among the most illuminating parts of the work. It is sometimes tempting to think that Barth belongs to that unfortunate class of teachers who are better at expounding other people's thoughts than putting over their own. Certainly, he does the former much more concisely and directly. But to say this would be to damn with faint praise. It would ignore all that Barth has said and said well, and forget all the forgotten truth that Barth has brought to light in fifty years of writing.

In the last analysis Barth's significance cannot be measured by his skill as a writer. Neither can it be assessed in terms of success or lack of it in forming a Barthian school. If there are Barthians (as undoubtedly there are), Karl Barth repeatedly protests that he is not one of them. From first to last his real concern is to point men to God in Christ. If they respond, the glory is God's. If they reject the call, the responsibility for doing so is theirs. The real worth of a minister and a theologian does not depend on the number of heads that can be counted but upon his loyalty to his calling.

In a sense the theologian is like a sparring partner. His job is to keep the church on its toes both intellectually and spiritually. If the church neglects truth, sooner or later it will get flabby and go sick; and what once were soul-stirring insights will degenerate into hollow platitudes. And if the church neglects its call to live out the gospel as the people of God, then whatever truth the church has will go sour on it. We may think that there are places where Barth goes sadly wrong. This essay is at least in part an attempt to point these out. But no-one with any first-hand acquaintance with his writings can deny Barth's zeal and sense of vocation in calling men in general and the church in particular back to God.

What then can we learn from Barth? In this chapter I want to draw together the main points of my discussion. For convenience I shall group them together under the headings of chapters 2, 3 and 4.

I THE WORD OF GOD AND THE KNOWLEDGE OF GOD
a. Barth's perspective
In the first place, Barth puts theology in its right perspective. Theology is not an intellectual exercise for those with a special flair. Nor is it a hobby for those with a mind to indulge themselves in it. Theology concerns the whole church for it is concerned with the Word of God to man. It is a matter of life and death. It touches every department of our lives.

In a sense everyone has his own theology; we all have some ideas about God and man. But not everyone has a true theology. This lay behind Barth's first and perhaps greatest discovery of the reality of the Word of God in those early years as a pastor at Safenwil. Knowledge of God is a gift of God. It is a characteristic of modern men – and not least of many modern so-called theologians – that they behave as if they have got God in their pockets. We talk so glibly about Him. We presume to sit in judgment. Whatever its faults and however much Barth himself felt the need to revise its way of putting things, Barth's commentary on Romans puts man back in his place. It reminds us of the One with whom we all have to do. It tells us bluntly that so much of our religion is a sham, a barrier of our own devising, designed to stop us from encountering the living God.

There are those who would like to explain away this aspect of Barth as a pessimistic hangover from all the horrors of World War I. Those who say this have yet to learn to know themselves. They have yet to get to grips with the message of the Bible.

It would be easy for those who have been brought up on an evangelical diet to adopt a we-have-known-that-all-along attitude. But Barth came to these insights from a background steeped in a man-centred liberalism. He reached them only after a hard, uphill battle. He proclaimed them in a prophetic way. And there are many things that Barth has to say, as he does in his *Evangelical Theology: An Introduction,* on the place in the Christian life of wonder, concern, commitment, prayer, study, service and love which all Christians need to hear and hear again.

But apart from the attitude with which we approach theology, Barth is surely right in the way he binds knowledge of God to the Word of God. Only God can reveal God. If we want to know God, we must start where God starts. We must begin not with our preconceived ideas but with God's revelation of Himself in His Word. There are those who accuse Barth of committing intellectual suicide because of his teaching on revelation. They would like some objective, rational proof of God over and above the revelation that comes through Christ and the gospel. But in the nature of the case there can be no proof apart from revelation. God would not be God if there were. The Word of God brings with it its own proof. As we said when discussing the question: How do we know that the Bible is the Word of God?, the argument may be circular, but it is not viciously so.[1] In point of fact, the boot is (to change the metaphor) on the other foot. If God reveals Himself in a certain way, it is intellectual (and spiritual) suicide to ignore what God has

[1] See above, pp. 36ff., *cf.* pp. 92f.

given, and to demand proofs that are not there. Genuine scientific method begins with the evidence that is there. It is concerned with what is given, not with what is not. Every science is shaped by its object. The nature of the data concerned decides the method of approach. So it is with theology. And to that extent Barth's theology is a genuine science.[2] It is not a piece of arbitrary irrationalism. His work stands or falls as an attempt to grapple with the reality to which the Bible points: God's revelation of Himself in His Word written and incarnate.

b. Revelation and the Bible

Barth's view of the Bible has come under fire from both the conservative and the liberal flanks. The chief conservative complaint has been that Barthianism fails to do justice to the God-given, inspired character of the Scriptures. It appears to drive a wedge between revelation on the one hand and the Bible on the other. Whereas Barth seems to relegate the status of the Bible by calling it a *witness* to revelation, the Scriptures themselves claim to be the Word of God written. Certainly this latter view was that of Jesus Himself.[3] And a close examination of what the Bible itself says about revelation, inspiration and the Word of God leads to the same conclusion.[4]

At certain points we have noted that the gap between Barth and this older orthodox view of the Bible which was held almost universally by Christians until the advent of theological liberalism is narrower than is sometimes imagined. When Barth's view of this or that comes under discussion, the first question to ask is: Which Barth? The Barth of 1966 should not be saddled with all the views of the Barth of 1916 or 1926. The Barth we must reckon with is the Barth of the *Church Dogmatics* and the other later works. Otherwise, we are playing with an Aunt Sally. This is

[2] See above, p. 29, n. 4; *cf.* pp. 92f.
[3] *Cf.* J. W. Wenham, *Our Lord's View of the Old Testament* (Tyndale Press, 1953, I.V.F., 1964²).
[4] *Cf.* B. B. Warfield, *The Inspiration and Authority of the Bible* (Marshall, Morgan and Scott, 1951); J. I. Packer, *'Fundamentalism' and the Word of God* (I.V.F., 1958), pp. 41–114.

particularly true when it comes to questions of revelation. For here the mature Barth (as distinct from Barth the Dialectical Theologian) has not only recovered the insights of the older orthodoxy but has also broken new ground.

Evangelicals regard the Bible as the Word of God, spoken at different times through different men and now written down and collected together. Liberals see it as a collection of documents, often fallible but which nevertheless contain profound insights. At first glance Karl Barth seems to stand somewhere between the two. Certainly he began with the presuppositions of the liberals. But from his first pastorate onwards his mind began to change. His new starting-point, the great discovery of his early ministry, was the fact that God today still speaks through the Bible. This is something quite different from saying that the writers of Scripture had some very remarkable insights into life. The key to Barth's understanding of the Bible is the fact that God reveals Himself in a unique way through these writings.

When Barth is asked what proof he has of this, his reply is that we must repeat the same experiment for ourselves. In the nature of the case this is the only proof that can count. We miss the point, if we try to interpret the Barth of the *Church Dogmatics* as a piece of pseudo-philosophy disguised as biblical theology. The central doctrine of Barth's teaching on revelation is the biblical one that revelation is none other than God revealing Himself. Revelation, Barth rightly says, is not something separate from God. It is God Himself in action. Barth's attitude to the Bible stands or falls as an analysis of what this involves.

Barth's distinction between the three *forms* of the Word of God[5] can be helpful. On the one hand, it is a reminder that in the strictest sense of the term Christ is the Word of God. He is the One who reveals God to man. On the other hand, it indicates the way that the Scriptures and preaching (as the two secondary *forms* of the Word of God) are related to Christ and to each other. The Scriptures bear witness to Christ in the biblical sense of the term (*cf.* John 5:39). As we receive their witness, we encounter Him to whom they bear witness. Their witness is, moreover, a specially

[5] See above, pp. 30–35.

commissioned witness. The writers of Scripture stand in a special relation to God. We cannot side-step them and find an alternative route to Him. Nor may we pick and choose what we want to believe of their message. For God speaks through the whole of it. It is at our peril that we neglect any part. It is by the Scriptures that we come to Christ, or rather that Christ comes to us. It is by them that we must test all our preaching, speaking and thinking about God.

It is in this way that Barth comes to speak of the inspiration of Scripture.[6] His view is a far cry from the old-fashioned liberal one that took inspiration to mean no more than inspiring. On the basis of it Barth could even endorse the view of Augustine, that what Scripture says God says.[7] There is, however, a difference of emphasis between Barth and traditional orthodoxy. Barth's stress falls on the reality of God's revelation of Himself through Scripture. Evangelicalism has come to stress the latter's God-given authority. The two points are really complementary, and should not be played off against each other. There are, however, three significant differences which deserve mention.

Whereas Barth acknowledges the authority and inspired character of the Scriptures, his handling of the evidence is nowhere near so thorough as that of (say) the American scholar, B. B. Warfield, in the opening decades of the century, whose numerous articles on the subject were collected and published under the title *The Inspiration and Authority of the Bible*. As a consequence, despite its enormous length Barth's treatment of the Word of God is not nearly so exact as it might have been. The serious student on the subject of authority will have to look beyond Barth for a complete picture.

On the other hand (and in the second place), Barth's suggestive handling of the nature of religious truth takes the discussion a stage beyond that at which it was debated by the men of Warfield's generation. As was said above,[8] Barth's teaching on analogy has real bearing on the current debates between the philosophers and theologians on the

---

[6] See above, pp. 54–62.   [7] *Confessions*, XIII, 29.
[8] See above, pp. 47–54.

nature, status and function of language. Until recently the discussion was largely confined to academic circles. But it is bound to filter through to the non-professional who is nevertheless concerned with religious questions. Henceforth books dealing with questions of authority and revelation will not be able to ignore it. And what Barth has to say on this score gives a valuable lead.

But thirdly, Barth's doctrine of revelation and authority has an Achilles' heel which has not gone unnoticed by conservative and liberal theologians. We have seen how Barth comes to regard the Bible as the revealing Word of God. We have suggested that his view has much in common with that of evangelicalism and traditional orthodoxy. But whereas for the latter the fact that God speaks through the Bible meant that it is entirely dependable, Barth hesitates to draw the same conclusion. Although he refuses to play off one part of Scripture against another, he nevertheless speaks of the Bible's *capacity for errors*.[9] In other words, we are presented with the intolerable dilemma that the Bible is at least *in theory* true and false at the same time. It is true in so far as God speaks through it. But it may be false in so far as the same passage may be factually wrong. The words *in theory* are used advisedly, because in practice Barth seems to duck the issue. Having made his concession to his critical background, Barth reverts to what looks like an uncritical view of the Bible. But the problem is a real one. Barth himself is too perceptive a theologian to go for the usual escape-route of those who want the best of both worlds and say that the Bible contains some parts which are inspired and others which are not. For neither the testimony of the Bible itself to its own character nor Barth's own experience as a Christian allows this. God speaks through the whole—admittedly in many different ways, but nevertheless through the whole. What Barth does is to hand us back the problem disguised as the solution. But it is impossible to maintain high doctrines of revelation and inspiration without at the same time being willing to defend the veracity and historicity of the biblical writings. This is something which Barth

[9] See above, pp. 56ff.

neglects to do, but which is by no means incompatible with the main thrust of his teaching. Indeed, it is an important corollary of it.

To sum up on Barth's approach to revelation and the Bible, it is clear that Barth has not said the last word. His treatment leaves loose ends and gaping holes. But it does not deserve to be written off as a piece of cryptic philosophy, as some Evangelicals do. Barth is often suggestive and penetrating. He brings to light questions all too often left in semi-obscurity. As he himself would want to say, each point of his teaching should be treated strictly on merit.

c. Barth's doctrine of the Trinity

The same may be said of Barth's approach to the doctrine of the Trinity.[1] His terminology may or may not be an advance upon the traditional terms. But Barth's teaching stands out in an age where it is regularly suggested that the doctrine itself is little more than a combination of scholastic ingenuity and semi-pagan philosophy. The doctrine of the Trinity is not a sort of optional extra. It arises directly from our encounter with God. Barth's teaching on the Trinity is not only a penetrating analysis of New Testament teaching. It is a powerful reminder of the One with whom we as men all have to do.

II THE BANKRUPTCY OF NATURAL THEOLOGY

It would be tedious and unnecessary to outline once again Barth's reasons for rejecting natural theology. Barth rejects natural theology because it is a dead end. God has revealed Himself in Christ. Revelation is a matter of grace. It is through the gospel that men come to a knowledge of God. By contrast the arguments of the natural theologians never quite add up to a solid knowledge of the living God. There is always something missing.

We saw this first in the debate between Barth and Brunner in the early thirties.[2] Brunner was pleading for a fresh approach to the subject. He listed various points which suggested a lead. At first they looked promising, and at times Barth overstated his case. But Brunner's arguments had an

[1] See above, pp. 67–76.   [2] See above, pp. 78–88.

unfortunate habit of fizzling out at the crucial point. And in the end, nothing that Brunner said – however true it may have been in itself – turned out to offer a suitable basis. We then turned to the traditional arguments for the existence of God to see whether these enabled one to build up a coherent knowledge of God without recourse to the Christian revelation.[3] In each case we saw that the arguments fell far short of what they were intended to do. Finally we returned to the question of whether there is a revelation of God in nature.[4] Here the conclusion was reached that common experience and important strands of biblical teaching point to the fact that man in himself is aware of God. This awareness is not enough to build a whole theology upon. But it is a profound awareness of One with whom man has to do.

If this reasoning is valid there must follow certain profound consequences for the church in its task of bringing its message to the world. In our sceptical modern age where it is more fashionable to express agnosticism than faith, it is tempting for the church to try to find neutral common ground on which it can build up 'objective' proofs of God. But all too often what men need is not some common ground but to have their bluff called. It is not proof that men need. In their heart of hearts they are aware of God already. The church does no service either to the world or to itself if it permits itself to get side-tracked into arguments that do not really work. In this situation what it needs above all is to have the courage of its convictions. It must let the Christian message speak for itself and bring with it its own point of contact.

This is not the same as saying that any old gospel sermon will do for each and every occasion. Preaching the gospel is not a matter of grinding out the same familiar texts to all and sundry. When Jesus and the prophets spoke, they spoke to men as they were, all with their own particular needs. They told them what they needed. They brought a message from God. Because their words came from God they carried conviction and reached men's hearts. The great need of the church today is to hear again the Word of God, to apply

[3] See above, pp. 88–91.   [4] See above, pp. 94–98.

it to itself and bring it to the world. This is the challenge that Karl Barth presents to the church in the twentieth century. It is a call to the people of God to live by the Word of God.

III BARTH'S CHRIST-CENTRED APPROACH TO GOD, CREATION AND RECONCILIATION

In chapter 4 we turned to Barth's interpretation of three major themes: the nature of God, creation, and reconciliation. In theological circles there is an awareness that Barth has something of real importance to say here, but it is an awareness that is tinged by a feeling that grave defects are concealed behind the impressive façade. G. W. Bromiley, co-editor of the English edition of Barth's *Church Dogmatics*, has taken this up in a recent study of Barth.[5] He asks whether there might not be some 'comprehensive error' which has cast a shadow over the whole of Barth's thinking.[6] He mentions Cornelius Van Til whose works *The New Modernism* and *Christianity and Barthianism* have argued that Barth's thought is vitiated from top to bottom by alien, non-Christian philosophic presuppositions. Yet Van Til's study is often so strained that Barth himself feels that it is more a wilful caricature than a serious discussion. In *The Triumph of Grace in the Theology of Karl Barth*, G. C. Berkouwer suggests that the overruling concept in Barth's teaching is that of the idea of triumphant grace. Certainly the two elements of divine sovereignty and overflowing grace are present. All Barth's thinking is coloured by his conception of them. But whilst Berkouwer's study is thoughtful and detailed, it runs counter, as Barth himself has pointed out,[7] to the main thrust of his teaching. For it substitutes an abstract idea for the person of Jesus Christ as the basis and centre of Barth's thought. Bromiley then turns to the suggestion that Christomonism might be 'perhaps a more valid description'.[8] But this too falls wide of the mark. On the one hand, it does violence to the Trinitarian basis of Barth's thinking. And on the other, it is perverse to

---

[5] 'Karl Barth' in *Creative Minds in Contemporary Theology*, edited by Philip Edgcumbe Hughes (Eerdmans, Grand Rapids, 1966), pp. 27–59.
[6] *Op. cit.*, p. 52.   [7] *C.D.*, IV, 3, pp. 173f.   [8] *Op. cit.*, p. 52.

suggest that Barth reduces everything to a single, ultimate substance or principle.

Bromiley reluctantly concludes that 'A master key to Barth's weaknesses might resolve many problems, but it is hard to feel much confidence in those suggested'.[9] Nevertheless, each of those keys so far suggested has some element of truth. And if the analysis of this study is correct, there is an underlying unity in Barth's thinking. In a sense Barth's theology is like Elgar's *Enigma Variations*. All his teaching is a series of variations upon the same simple, basic theme. We have tried to express it by saying that for Barth all God's dealings with men are effected in and through the person of Jesus Christ. And since God is sovereign, loving and gracious, man's whole being in Christ is caught up in this love and grace. The theme was sounded as early as the First World War when Barth wrote his commentary on Romans. Here Christ the revealing Word was depicted as the sole revelation of God. He alone is the light of this dark world. The theme was developed in the *Church Dogmatics*, but in essentials it remained the same. There is a sense in which even the Bible is not a revelation but only the *witness* to the unique revelation that is in Christ. This emphasis on Christ is also the key to Barth's rejection of natural theology. All revelation of God comes through Christ. It is a waste of time to look for it elsewhere.

In our last main chapter we noticed a shift of emphasis. Barth did not reject what he had written earlier. The old emphasis on the sovereign freedom of God remains. Barth still stands by his teaching on God's free revelation of Himself in His Word. But as he turned from the subject of the revealer to that of what is revealed, Barth's interest shifted from the revealing Word to the Word incarnate. As it did so, he saw a union of God and man implied in the union of divine and human nature in the person of Jesus Christ. To this union he gave the biblical name of the *covenant*.[1] And in the light of the *covenant* Barth reshaped the entire Christian message.

In view of the *covenant* Barth makes election 'the sum of the Gospel', for in the union of the humanity and

<hr />

[9] *Ibid.*   [1] See above, pp. 99–102.

divinity of Christ God has bound the whole of humanity
to Himself.[2] In choosing Jesus Christ, God has chosen mankind to be His covenant partner. This is the very key to
understanding the divine nature.[3] For this is the most
important thing about God. God would not be God without
the *covenant*. It is also the key to creation. For man is above
all the covenant partner of God. The world and the universe
came into being because of the *covenant*.[4] Moreover, we
only know what man is when we see him in the light of the
covenant.[5] When Barth turns to the question of sin, he sees
it basically as a reaction against the *covenant*.[6]

The reconciliation effected by Christ on the cross is interpreted by the same principle. Christ has died for all men
absolutely.[7] Because God deals with all men through Christ
and all men are in Christ already, all are reconciled. The
law of God comes to all men as *fulfilled* law, for Christ has
fulfilled it for all.[8] The difference between the believer and
the unbeliever is that the believer knows that he has been
reconciled, whereas the unbeliever has yet to come to realize
it. He is still trying to live the life of the unreconciled. The
same principle brings Barth to the brink of universalism,
but he stops short at the last moment.[9] Instead of following
through the logic of concluding that all men will be saved,
since all have been reconciled, Barth ventures to suggest that
some may possibly still try to live the life of the unreconciled throughout eternity, even though this is fundamentally
impossible.

We have not pursued Barth's thought in all its ramifications. But we have examined its main outlines in some
detail. No-one can deny that it has a beautifully worked out
symmetry. At the same time it has a profound simplicity. All
God's dealings with men are effected in and through Jesus
Christ through whom grace triumphs over all. Barth has
far surpassed all his predecessors in making his theology
Christ-centred. But this, its apparent strength, is in fact its
real weakness. At many points (as we saw in the case of

---

[2] See above, pp. 100–103, 113ff.
[3] See above, pp. 108ff.
[4] See above, pp. 110–113.
[5] See above, pp.113–119.
[6] See above, pp. 119–123.
[7] See above, pp. 124ff.
[8] See above, pp. 126-130.
[9] See above, pp. 130-133.

Barth's treatment of revelation) this Christ-centredness has
led Barth to real insights. But at other points it is artificial
and forced. In the last chapter we looked at Barth's Christological approach from opposite ends. We began by examining its foundation in the idea of the *covenant* and the New
Testament teaching about Christ.[1] We then looked at the
opposite end, as it were, and saw where it all led in the light
of Barth's teaching on judgment and justification.[2] In each
case we were obliged to conclude that Barth had used his
basic Christological principle like a Procrustean bed. Some
important aspects of New Testament teaching had to be
stretched to make them fit, while others had to be lopped
off. Despite his protests that he is not concerned with a
Christ-principle but with Christ Himself,[3] we have been
obliged to conclude that it is a Christ-idea that often gives
Barth his characteristic emphases. We cannot remain true
to the witness of the New Testament, and follow Barth in
his Christocentric programme. For whilst God deals with
men through Christ, Christ is not equally all things to all
men. To those who respond to God's love He is Saviour;
but to those who reject it He is Judge. According to the
witness of the New Testament, God deals with men in two
ways. He deals with them as they are in themselves, and He
deals with them as they are in Christ. The two spheres are
not identical. They overlap. All men are by nature in the
first. Some are by grace in the second.

In saying this, as we said before, we are not saying anything that is new. It is the great common theme of Christian
teaching down the ages. It is the central message of the
Bible. The real significance of Karl Barth is that he has
brought these fundamental questions back into the centre
of attention. He has not only done this; he has brought
into focus the basic issues which decide the answer to
these questions. Thus, he has not only challenged the
church to think again about questions like: How do we
know God? How does man stand with God? Barth puts to us
the questions: What part does Christ play in revelation?
What is the nature of religious truth? Is the Bible our only

---

[1] See above, pp. 101–108; *cf.* pp. 113–117.   [2] See above, pp. 130–139.
[3] *C.D.*, IV, 3, p. 174.

source of knowledge about God? What factors determine our relationship with God? He has also raised again key themes of the Bible which are regularly pushed into the background in the church today – themes like judgment, the reconciliation not only of man to God but of God to man, and the covenant as the underlying principle of God's dealings with men.

In all this Barth has things to say which are of positive value. But there is also much that needs qualification and restatement if we are to remain true to the source and standard which Barth himself acknowledges as the criterion of Christian thinking, Holy Scripture. The way forward to a deeper understanding of the Christian message lies therefore neither in a wholesale acceptance nor in a wholesale rejection of what he has to say. It lies rather with the way we treat the issues that he has raised. In the last analysis, it depends, as Barth himself would say, upon our willingness to hear the Word of God.

A NOTE ON BOOKS

Karl Barth has published over 500 books, papers, sermons and articles. Details of his major writings will be found above on pages 14–29. A bibliography complete to the end of 1955 has been compiled by Ch. von Kirschbaum and appears in the volume published to celebrate Barth's seventieth birthday in 1956, *Antwort*, pp. 945–960. This has been brought up to date by Eberhard Busch in the parallel volume marking his eightieth birthday, *Parrhesia*, pp. 709–723. These lists include translations into many languages.

Works on Barth published before the war tend to be obsolete or of limited interest in view of Barth's drastic later developments. At best they take in no more than the first part of the first volume of the *Church Dogmatics*. Thus H. R. Mackintosh's *Types of Modern Theology: Schleiermacher to Barth* (Nisbet, 1937; now a Fontana paperback) is useful for the earlier Barth and Barth's predecessors, but its total picture is obviously very incomplete.

The two best general introductions to Barth are Herbert Hartwell, *The Theology of Karl Barth: An Introduction* (Duckworth, 1964) and G. C. Berkouwer, *The Triumph of Grace in the Theology of Karl Barth*, Eng. tr. by Harry R. Boer (Paternoster, 1956). Hartwell is lucid, concise and yet detailed. It is written in a friendly but not uncritical spirit. Barth himself has described Berkouwer's book as a 'great book on myself',[1] although he disagrees with the suggestion that an abstract idea like the triumph of grace is really the key thought of his theology.[2] The book has certain disadvantages. Page references are given to the German edition

[1] *C.D.*, IV, 2, p. xii.   [2] *C.D.*, IV, 3, pp. 173f.

of Barth, and his layout which involves some repetition does not make it too easy to grasp Barth's basic ideas. However, it contains a full and fair critique, written from a conservative evangelical standpoint. Although it does not really deal with Barth on revelation, it exposes the strengths and weaknesses of his later teaching.

Two books attempt to set out Barth's teaching in précis form. Otto Weber, *Karl Barth's Church Dogmatics: An Introductory Report on Volumes I: 1 to III: 4* (Lutterworth, 1953) is a detailed, almost page-by-page analysis, threading sentences of Barth's on to a string of the author's own narrative. The current German edition includes Barth's teaching on reconciliation. *Karl Barth: Church Dogmatics. A Selection with Introduction* by Helmut Gollwitzer, translated and edited by G. W. Bromiley (T. & T. Clark, 1961) is a valuable paperback anthology of extracts arranged under key headings. An introductory essay seeks to set them in the context of Barth's life and thought. An inevitable drawback of both volumes is that, whilst they map out Barth's teaching on a wide range of topics, they are inclined to leave out the argument and motivation which have led Barth to the conclusions that he holds. And inevitably there is no critical evaluation.

A. B. Come, *An Introduction to Barth's Dogmatics for Preachers* (S.C.M. Press, 1963) is the work of an American scholar who spent the best part of a year working on Barth under Barth. In parts it is a bit like listening to an American visitor to Europe telling the folks back home what a swell little place it is. But it has many valuable features, not the least being the sketch of Barth's life which has been vetted by Barth himself. It contains a conducted tour around the *Church Dogmatics*. But its main aim is to ask what the average minister can learn from Barth for his preaching.

Cornelius Van Til has written two large books on Barth and several critical studies. His writings are not the easiest of introductions for the beginner. They criticize Barth in the light of what Van Til sees to be Barth's alien, non-Christian philosophical presuppositions. These are contrasted with what Van Til regards as valid presuppositions for Christian thinking. The critique is sometimes penetrating. But it often appears to take much for granted, not least what Barth actually says and also the biblical exegesis which Van Til claims to underlie his own thought. The earlier book, *The New Modernism: An Appraisal of the Theology of Barth and Brunner* (James Clarke, 1946) is largely concerned with revelation. *Christianity and Barthianism* (Presbyterian and Reformed Publishing Co., 1962) goes on to include Barth's later thought. A valuable feature of this book is Van Til's critiques of many Protestant and Catholic scholars and their views on Barth. In both works Van Til is concerned to press Barth to the logical, philosophical conclusions that he finds inherent in his thought.

G. W. Bromiley gives a brief, all-round survey and critique in his study of Karl Barth in *Creative Minds in Contemporary Theology*, edited by Philip Edgcumbe Hughes (Eerdmans, Grand Rapids, 1966), pp. 27–59. Those interested in trends in modern theology will find this volume generally useful. They will be able to compare Barth's teaching with that of his contemporaries on the continent, in England and the United States. The book contains thirteen studies of modern theologians, including Berkouwer, Brunner and Bultmann. Barth's approach is contrasted with that of Nygren and Bultmann by the Scandinavian Lutheran theologian, Gustaf Wingren, in his *Theology in Conflict: Nygren, Barth, Bultmann,* Eng. tr. by E. H. Wahlstrom (Oliver & Boyd, 1958). Some of his criticisms find their mark, but others seem a bit wild. And the study does not claim to be exhaustive.

There are several important books which deal with limited aspects of Barth. T. F. Torrance, *Karl Barth: An Introduction to his Early Theology, 1910-1931* (S.C.M. Press, 1962) is the most important study in English of Barth's early years and of Dialectical Theology. It breaks off, however, at the point where Barth was beginning his life's main work. A fascinating background supplement to this early period is the correspondence of Barth and his life-long friend, Eduard Thurneysen. This has been previously published in the original German partly in *Antwort*, pp. 831–864 and partly in *Gottesdienst – Menschendienst: Eduard Thurneysen zum 70. Geburtstag* (Evangelischer Verlag, Zollikon, 1958), pp. 7–173. It now appears in English in the translation of James D. Smart under the title *Revolutionary Theology in the Making; Barth–Thurneysen Correspondence, 1914–1925* (Epworth, 1964).

Gordon H. Clark, *Karl Barth's Theological Method* (Presbyterian and Reformed Publishing Co., Philadelphia, 1963) is a good discussion of the subject so far as it goes. But it confines itself largely to the teaching on revelation and the Bible as set out in the first volume of Barth's *Church Dogmatics*. It does not touch at all on Barth's view of the incarnation and covenant which are of crucial importance for Barth's theological method in dealing with the content of theology – the doctrines of God, creation and reconciliation. Barth's approach to Scripture is very sympathetically dealt with by J. K. S. Reid in *The Authority of Scripture: A Study of the Reformation and Post-Reformation Understanding of the Bible* (Methuen, 1957) which is helpful in comparing Barth with Brunner and setting him in historical context. It is less so in setting out the evangelical view. Further background material is given by H. D. McDonald in his two books, *Ideas of Revelation: An Historical Study A.D. 1700 to A.D. 1860* (Macmillan, 1959) and *Theories of Revelation: An Historical Study, 1860–1960* (Allen and Unwin, 1963). An important early study was F. W. Camfield's London D.D. thesis, *Revelation and the Holy Spirit: An Essay in Barthian Theology* (Elliot Stock, 1933). Mention may also be made of Alan Fairweather, *The Word as Truth: A Critical Examination of the Christian Doctrine of Revelation in the Writings of Thomas Aquinas and Karl Barth* (Lutterworth, 1944). But the most thorough, up-to-date critique of Barth's teaching on revelation is one written from an evangelical standpoint, Klaas Runia's *Karl Barth's Doctrine of Holy Scripture* (Eerdmans, Grand Rapids, 1962). This important study is valuable not only for its treatment of Barth but as a contribution in its own right to our understanding of revelation and the Bible.

Barth's teaching on the Trinity is touched upon briefly by R. S. Franks in his outline history *The Doctrine of the Trinity* (Duckworth, 1958). The most detailed study to date is that of Claude Welch in *The Trinity in Contemporary Theology* (S.C.M. Press, 1953) which is valuable for comparing Barth's approach with that of contemporaries like Leonard Hodgson. Fred H. Klooster, *The Significance of Barth's Theology: An Appraisal with Special Reference to Election and Reconciliation* (Baker, Grand Rapids, 1963) contains three brief but lucid lectures on the subjects indicated. They are written from an evangelical standpoint.

Barth's teaching has also attracted the attention of Roman Catholic writers. A major study now available in English is that by Hans Küng on *Justification: The Doctrine of Karl Barth and a Catholic Reflection,* Eng. tr. by T. Collins, E. E. Tolk and O. Grandskou (Burns & Oates, 1966). This widely hailed work not only seeks to set Barth's teaching on the subject in the context of his thought; it argues that Catholic and Protestant teaching on justification (especially Barth's) come much closer to each other than is commonly supposed. *Grace Versus Nature: Studies in Karl Barth's Church Dogmatics* (Sheed & Ward, 1965) is the work of a British Roman Catholic philosopher, Hugo Meynell. It is partly a defence of natural theology and partly a study of Barth's teaching on creation and reconciliation.

Readers interested in particular aspects of Barth's thought will find it useful to go through the back numbers of the *Scottish Journal of Theology* and also consult its *Occasional Papers.* It is impossible here to give a complete list, but the reader will easily be able to find for himself the surveys of the individual volumes of the *Church Dogmatics* that have been made as the volumes were published. Mention might also be made of articles like F. W. Camfield's 'Man in his Time' (Vol. 3, 1950, pp. 127–148) and Barth's own reflections on his vocation (Vol. 14, 1961, pp. 225–228). John D. Godsey's *Karl Barth's Table Talk* (*S.J.T. Occasional Papers No. 10*) contains dialogue between Barth and his students on his teaching, based upon the author's analysis of the *Church Dogmatics.*

The present study has tried to avoid giving too many references to works in foreign languages. But there are several which deserve special mention. Two of the most important studies on Barth to be written yet are by Roman Catholic theologians: Hans Urs von Balthasar, *Karl Barth: Darstellung und Deutung seiner Theologie* (Hegner-

Bücherei im Summa Verlag, Olten, 1951, 1962²), and Henri Bouillard, *Karl Barth*, 3 volumes (Aubier, Paris, 1957). These works are indispensable to a serious, detailed study of Barth. Of less importance, but nevertheless worth mentioning, is another work by a Roman Catholic, J. Hamer, *Karl Barth: L'Occasionalisme Théologique de Karl Barth. Étude sur sa Méthode Dogmatique* (Desclée de Brouwer, Paris, 1949).

Last but by no means least are the various volumes published in honour of Barth to mark different birthdays. There are two massive volumes celebrating his seventieth and eightieth birthdays published in German. *Antwort. Karl Barth zum siebzigsten Geburtstag am 10. Mai 1956* (Evangelischer Verlag, Zollikon-Zürich, 1956) has three main sections. The first deals with aspects of Barth's work; the second with miscellaneous themes in part raised by Barth; the third with Barth himself as theologian, minister and man. *Parrhesia. Karl Barth zum achtzigsten Geburtstag am 10. Mai 1966* (same publishers) is largely the work of the younger generation of theologians on the continent. Their aim is not to repeat what was in the previous volume but to take up further themes raised by Barth in the course of his life and work. The comparable volumes in French and English have a similar scope: *Hommage et Reconnaissance. Recueil de travaux publiés à l'occasion du soixantième anniversaire de Karl Barth* (Delachaux & Niestlé, Neuchâtel and Paris, 1946); *Essays in Christology for Karl Barth*, edited by T. H. L. Parker (Lutterworth, 1956); and *Service in Christ*, also edited by T. H. L. Parker (Epworth, 1966).

INDEX